Earth Spirit

The Circle of Life
is Broken

An Eco-Spiritual Philosophy
of the Climate Crisis

Earth Spirit

The Circle of Life
is Broken

An Eco-Spiritual Philosophy
of the Climate Crisis

Brendan Myers

MOON
BOOKS
Winchester, UK
Washington, USA

JOHN HUNT PUBLISHING

First published by Moon Books, 2022
Moon Books is an imprint of John Hunt Publishing Ltd., No. 3 East Street, Alresford
Hampshire SO24 9EE, UK
office@jhpbooks.net
www.johnhuntpublishing.com
www.moon-books.net

For distributor details and how to order please visit the 'Ordering' section on our website.

Text copyright: Brendan Myers 2021

ISBN: 978 1 78904 977 0
978 1 78904 978 7 (ebook)
Library of Congress Control Number: 2021949892

A CIP catalogue record for this book is available from the British Library.

Design: Matthew Greenfield

UK: Printed and bound by CPI Group (UK) Ltd, Croydon, CR0 4YY
Printed in North America by CPI GPS partners

We operate a distinctive and ethical publishing philosophy in
all areas of our business, from our global network of authors to
production and worldwide distribution.

Contents

For my grandfather, Clarence Comfort. (1921-2022)

"Heaven is here on Earth. When we die, our reputation lives on. If it is good, then that is our Heaven or if it is bad then that is our hell... Life after death is the effect that we leave to those that follow."
--From his memoirs.

Acknowledgements

There's a lake near my house that I have come to think of as special and magical. The path to reach it goes through fields and forests, over rocky hills and muddy gullies: a few hours' adventure that I give to myself as often as I can. Some of the ideas that appear in this book came to me during those walks, and also during the hours I sat on the banks or the bluffs, contemplating the light upon the water. Thus, as strange as it may sound to some of you, I wish to thank that lake: its waters and shores, its vista, its peace. And I wish to thank all the life in the forest surrounding: every flower and tree, every critter and creature, every breeze, and the moon, and the sun.

I also have many friends to thank. The first of these are my students at Heritage College. They shall have to live with the climate crisis for all of their lives, no matter what anyone does. Prompted by their questions and anxieties about it, I added ecology to my History of Science curriculum in 2017. While preparing that curriculum, I hit upon a deeply troubling discovery, which appears as the title of a meditation in this book, and which got the process of writing underway. I also wish to thank my college's librarians, who taught me a few new research methods and tricks that I didn't know before.

I must also thank Trevor Greenfield, editor and general manager of Moon Books: a consistent support for my work for more than fifteen years. He asked me for a 20,000 word contribution to the Earth Spirit series, and then didn't bat an eye when I gave him a book more than three times longer. It's hard to imagine another publisher doing the same.

Three people read the first draft of this text. Their advice and observations were beyond valuable for pointing out errors, for suggesting new texts and authors to study, and for reminding me to consider more views than just my own. Thus I extend my gratitude to Giorgio Baruchello and Melinda Reidinger, friends and scholars with sharp minds and generous hearts. And I thank my partner Andrea Lobel, an excellent scholar herself, who provided not only many helpful remarks on the text, but also the moral and emotional support I needed while both studying ecological grief, and also feeling it.

Kenosis

The Overview Effect

Astronauts often describe the Earth as the most inviting and beautiful sight in all of space. Edgar Mitchell, the lunar module pilot on Apollo-14, said the sight of the Earth was like an "explosion of awareness," an "overwhelming sense of oneness and connectedness… accompanied by an ecstasy… an epiphany."[1] It is as if the Earth as a whole was only discovered by human beings in 1968, when Apollo-8 astronaut William Anders shot the famous Earthrise photograph: the image of the Earth coming out from behind the edge of the moon. In 1987 astronaut Frank White coined the word for the experience: *the overview effect*. Those who have experienced this view describe a sense of the unity of life, and of the Earth as a single organism. Some have even described the experience as religious.

"I had another feeling, that the earth is like a vibrant living thing. The vessels we've clearly seen on it looked like the blood and veins of human beings. I said to myself: this is the place we live, it's really magical." – Taikonaut Yang Liu.[2]

"…you look down and see the surface of that globe you've lived on all this time, and you know all those people down there and they are like you, they are you – and somehow you represent them… you recognize that you're a piece of this total life." – Astronaut Rusty Schweikart.[3]

"The feeling of unity is not simply an observation. With it comes a strong sense of compassion and concern for the state of our planet and the effect humans are having on it. It isn't important in which sea or lake you observe a slick of pollution or in the forests of which country a fire breaks out, or on which continent a hurricane arises. You are standing guard over the whole of our Earth." – Cosmonaut Yuri Artyushkin.[4]

My meditations in this book were prompted by the love I have felt for the various forests in which I grew up and in which I still dwell – a small scale version of the overview effect, perhaps, but it was *my* view, at least. I wanted to know what is it about my forest, and all the hillsides and meadows and oceans I have loved, which makes them so loveable. I wanted to know why I felt remorse, even grief, on the sight of my forest under stress: their leaves turning brown in July or August instead of October; animals and berry bushes and insects that were once abundant becoming scarce; bottles and food wrappings and other garbage left behind by tourists; seasons that once wheeled over the year in a familiar dance falling out of step.

When I was in primary school, I learned about species extinction, acid rain, the clearcutting of ancient rainforests in British Columbia, and the hole in the ozone layer. I learned of activists from groups like Greenpeace who interfered with whale hunters and nuclear bomb tests. I went on to study environmental philosophy at graduate school, where I tried to figure out what can be said to people who deny there's a climate crisis unfolding, or who admit there is a crisis but who claim it's a natural cycle, and in either case who argue that we don't need to do anything about it. In part I was motivated by the threat to my own forests, the landscapes of my childhood. But I was also motivated by what seemed to me a kind of stubborn incomprehension. Signs of global ecosystem breakdown were evident everywhere. People talked about them; responsible media agencies reported on them, sometimes in depth. Yet no one, or very few people, connected those signs to any larger reality. I wanted to know why.

For example, in the autumn of 2020, bird watchers in New

Mexico, Colorado, Texas, and various mid-west American states, reported whole flocks of migrating birds falling out of the sky, dead.[5] A researcher quoted in local media said: "the fact that it's happening... means that there's probably something more complex going on, and it might be a bit more challenging to control."[6] The 'something complex going on' is that the birds had to change their migration routes to avoid wildfires; water along the route had grown scarce; and insects had changed their usual habitats and breeding seasons, so the birds couldn't find them for food. For those reasons, the birds were dying in mid-flight from starvation. The largest of these die-offs happened during an out-of-season snowstorm in 2007: an estimated 1.5 million migrating birds died.[7] Migration routes which had taken centuries, perhaps millennia, to synchronize with dozens of environmental factors like weather patterns, the seasons, air currents, and the movements of other organisms, were breaking down.

But this was only one of many examples of global climate systems re-routing themselves as the greenhouse effect trapped more heat-energy in the oceans and the atmosphere. Birds, trees, plants, fish, insects, and other species unable to evolve fast enough to keep up with these changes, were dying. And again, hardly anyone I knew took notice. Even among those who did, hardly any of them commented on the relationships to other similar events.

One day, while I was drawing a diagram of a food web and meditating on it as if it was a mandala, the proposition struck me like a revelation: *the global circle of life is breaking down*. It isn't simply changing form. It is also short-circuiting; it is falling apart.

Several questions arose from that frightening proposition:

- What is the Circle of Life? (The answer is not as obvious as it may seem.)
- What becomes of the human reality when defined in relation to the circle of life?

• Can the Circle of Life be healed?

If these questions have to do with finding out whether or not the climate crisis is real, then this is a question for scientists. The general consensus of the scientists of the world is: *Yes, it's real.*[8] It is unprecedented in the last two thousand years. And many of its life-destructive effects are already irreversible.[9]

But if these questions have to do with the way we frame our reality as human beings, especially in the fields of human nature, freedom of the will, the future of civilization, and the meaning of life, then this is a question for philosophers like you and me.

These are very old philosophical questions, and they appear in several variations. They touch upon nearly every field of philosophical enquiry: our sources of knowledge, our moral decisions, our conception of reality, our feelings and emotions, our procedures of reasoning, our sense of identity. They are also questions of great practical urgency, as the climate crisis has the potential to disrupt if not destroy all our customary ways of living in relation to the earth, and to each other. For millennia we have taken for granted the stability of climates, the fertility and productivity of landscapes, the regular turning of the seasons, even the breathability of the air. This stability influenced some of our oldest religions and philosophies, especially those which posit a characteristic order and harmony for the universe. The ancient Egyptian concept of *Ma'at*, order and righteousness, to choose one example, was influenced by the regular and predictable annual flooding of the river Nile. The Jewish concept of justice, *Tzedakah* also depends on the idea that God created an orderly and harmonious universe. This idea was preserved in the Christian concept of charity, and the Islamic principle of *Zakat*. Because of the climate crisis, we might no longer be able to take the order and harmony of the world for granted as a basic assumption. Less theoretically, but no less meaningfully, some holiday songs like "I'm Dreaming Of A White Christmas" might make less sense in the future, when Christmas in the northern hemisphere comes with rain instead of snow.

Nor are Abrahamic religions the only ones affected. Wicca, Druidry, and related traditions use astronomical and ecological observations to mark the ritual festivals on the Eight-Fold Wheel of the Year. Those traditions have always been adaptable to local situations: Imbolc in Canada, for instance, is not a spring festival as it is in Ireland, because Canada in February is still up to its waist in snow. Nonetheless, the climate crisis will require that many neo-Pagan festival traditions shall have to change their meanings again. Religiously significant flowers, berries, animals, and foods might not be available "on time" for the festival where they once played important ritual roles. Heat waves, cold snaps, floods, and droughts, might make outdoor gatherings and camps more stressful, or impossible to hold at the customary sites. People who celebrated the Wheel of the Year as children or students forty years ago may not be able to pass on the same kind of celebration to their own children and students today. Thus the continuity of practice over time has come under threat, to the point where rituals and traditional practices must be re-invented every ten years or so. This in turn makes it harder to call them 'traditions' at all. The voice of the Goddess who says "I, who am the beauty of the green earth..."[10] might be hard to hear when the Earth is brown because of a drought, or grey and black from a forest fire.

The evidence of global ecosystem breakdown is readily available. To choose but one salient example: since the year 2000, the global average atmospheric concentration of carbon dioxide has risen by an average of twenty parts per million (ppm) every year; this is the fastest rate of increase in the last 800,000 years.[11] In May of 2018, the Mauna Loa Atmospheric Baseline Observatory detected a concentration of 411.25 ppm, the highest ever recorded up to that time.[12] In the 19th century, before the industrial revolution, global CO_2 concentration was about 280 ppm during warm periods, and about 180 during ice ages; the current rising trend is 100 times faster than any rising trend since the end of the last ice age, around 11,700 years ago.[13] The significance of these facts is not only that CO_2 has heat-retention properties which contribute to a global greenhouse effect. A human being exposed to CO_2 levels of 2,000 ppm or higher will experience nausea, headaches, disorientation, and insomnia. If that level became the global average, then we would lose the cognitive capacity to sustain civilization. At 5,000 ppm or higher, we die. And most air-breathing animals die with us.

Thus the question, 'How shall we face the earth, under the conditions of the climate crisis?', is not only of philosophical curiosity. It is also a question of life-or-death seriousness for all humanity, and for almost all life on Earth.

Yet there are several large, well-funded, and well-organised, and highly-visible forces in our society which denies the scientific research, or which casts unreasonable doubt upon it.[14] These forces would like us to continue to take the earth for granted, so that international capitalism, especially the oil industry, can carry on as usual.[15] Those forces have been so successful in shaping public opinion that four out of ten Americans deny the facts of climate change as a matter of political identity.[16] I suspect that this denial effort is also driven by the prospect that any *new* answer to the question, 'How shall we face the Earth?', will require us to change the arrangement of power-relations in our society, not only between human beings and the earth, but also between humanity's own divisions: wealth, nationality, gender, religion and culture, political identity, and so on. That is to say, any new answer to the root question might threaten those who benefit from the present arrangement of things. Those individuals are thus economically and politically incentivized to deny the reality of the climate crisis. As famously stated by Pulitzer-prize winning journalist Upton Sinclair, "It is difficult to get a man to understand something when his salary depends on his not understanding it."[17]

So I'm going to ask you to follow the arguments in this book as if you have nothing to lose by changing your beliefs. This might make it easier for you to evaluate the arguments by their own merits and flaws. As for my side of the bargain: I'll put forward the most reasonable arguments that I can. Reason, let me remind you, is neither hard, nor cold, nor without imagination; reason is organized curiosity. It tends not to be poetic. It is often uncomfortable, even disturbing. But when employed correctly, it has the great benefit of being right.

I have to get this right. Not "right for me"; not "right from my perspective" or some other empty relativism. No. There's too much riding on it: ecology, reality, time, space, civilization, and whether humanity will handle the climate crisis like a grown-up adult or whether we will fall, like the blind leading the blind, into stupidity and fascism and ecological disaster.

The Greening Of The Self Did Not Happen

Most college textbooks pin the start of environmental philosophy to the year 1949, when the American forestry professor Aldo Leopold proclaimed *The Land Ethic*, and the necessity to change "the role of Homo sapiens from conqueror of the land-community to plain member and citizen of it."[18] When I was an undergrad student in philosophy, Leopold's book, *A Sand County Almanac*, was taught as if it was the very first appearance of green philosophy anywhere in the history of the world. Of course, that's not true; people everywhere, and especially Indigenous peoples, had been thinking about the Earth and humanity's place in it for millennia. But at least in the Western philosophical tradition, the Earth, its place in human life, and our place in its life, was not considered problematic enough to warrant deep thinking until the twentieth century.

Leopold didn't build an *argument* for his Land Ethic. Rather, he said that his Land Ethic was inevitable: it was a logical next step in a continuing expansion of the moral sphere which, he said, has been happening for centuries:

> The extension of ethics, so far studied only by philosophers, is actually a process in ecological evolution. The first ethics dealt with the relation between individuals... Later accretions dealt with the relation between the individual and society... The extension of ethics to this third element in human environment is, if I read the evidence correctly, an evolutionary possibility and an ecological necessity. It is the third step in a sequence.[19]

Environmental thought in Europe begins earlier than Leopold, with Albert Schweitzer's 1923 book *Civilization And Ethics*, which introduces the principle of 'Reverence For Life'. This is the idea that "Ethics consists, therefore, in my experiencing the compulsion to show all will-to-live the same reverence as I do to my own."[20] All life, all living creatures and organisms, deserve care and respect, because, like you, they are alive and they express their will-to-life; there does not need to be any other reason. Like Leopold, Schweitzer believed that this expansion of the moral sphere was inevitable:

> It is the fate of every truth to be a subject for laughter until it is generally recognized. Once it was considered folly to assume that men of colour were really men and ought to be treated as such, but the folly has become an accepted truth. To-day it is thought to be going too far to declare that constant regard for everything that lives, down to the lowest manifestations of life, is a demand made by rational ethics. The time is coming, however, when people will be astonished that mankind needed so long a time to learn to regard thoughtless injury to life as incompatible with ethics.[21]

Another European, Hans Jonas, added that it is not only life and living organisms that deserve this reverence. It's also the environmental systems they live in. In *The Phenomenon of Life* (1966) he wrote that:

> Organism is seen as primarily determined by the conditions of its existence, and life is understood in terms of the organism-environment situation rather than in terms of the exercise of an autonomous nature. Organism and environment together form a system, and this hence-forth determines the basic concept of life.[22]

Since life is a *complex* system as opposed to a merely complicated one,[23] we cannot always predict what consequences will follow from our interference with life. It follows, Jonas argued, that we ought not to interfere, or if some interference cannot be avoided then it must be as light as possible. Jonas thought the logical foundation of ethics lay in the claim that humanity deserves a future. His ultimate moral norm, in this regard, is that we all ought to "act so that the effects of your action are compatible with the permanence of genuine human life."[24] Yet he still considers this goal an environmental one, because it is "grounded in the breadth of being, not merely in the singularity or oddness of man"; it requires that "we must learn from an interpretation of reality as a whole, [or] at least from an interpretation of life as a whole".[25] In terms of the expansion of the moral sphere into ecology, Jonas is a lateral step, rather than a forward advance; but it's a helpful step, nonetheless.

In 1970, American law professor and polemicist Charles Reich announced *The Greening Of America.* "There is a revolution coming", he said, and that this revolution would involve the "recovery" and "greening" of the individual self, then local communities, then larger and larger groups, and finally the whole body-politic of America. He argued that industrial, technology-intensive, and consumer-conformist society, which he called "the Machine" and "the Corporate State", produced in young people of his time a loss of self: "Beginning with school, if not before, an individual is systematically stripped of his imagination, his creativity, his heritage, his dreams, and his personal uniqueness, in order to style him into a productive unit for a mass, technological society."[26] The escape from the Machine, Reich says, is "the full hippie life, an attempt to live as if the Corporate State did not exist and some new form of community was already here," and that this new form of community was:

> ...an effort to restore, protect, and foster human consciousness. It [this effort] is most important because its aim is nothing less than to restore man's awareness of himself, of other people, of nature, of his own life. It seeks to make man, in everything that he does or experiences, more alive."[27]

Reich may not have been the first to frame environmental and cultural problems as having to do with selfhood and identity. Nonetheless, his particular way of framing those problems became the touchstone in the discourse. Before Reich, the questions were: 'What should I do? How should I live?' After Reich, they became, 'Who am I? What kind of person do I want to be? What kind of world will allow me to be truly myself?'

Thus in 1986, Norwegian philosopher Arne Naess declared that the ultimate ethical norm of Deep Ecology was "Self-realization!". The ecological processes which create the oxygen we breathe, grow the food we eat, purify the water, and absorb our waste, are so integrated into the functioning of a healthy human body that they can be conceived as extensions of the body, and therefore extensions of the self. So, when Naess declares "Self-realization!" as an ultimate moral value, he means this extended self, this ecological self. That's not only your body and your mind. It's also everything around you that makes it possible for you to be you: the recycling of your air and water, the growth of the plants and animals you eat, the growth of the things they eat, and so on, extending across all the land, the sea, and the sky. The realization of this extended self is, for Naess, both a moral postulate in its own right, and also a basic premise to support the argument that the destruction of the environment must end. For if we damage or disrupt the functioning of the extended self, we will damage or disrupt our own lives in turn. Ecological knowledge and environmental protection, he argued, is thus a kind of self-interest. The Greening of the Self was a process of individuals and societies coming to understand those principles, and entering a healthier relationship with the environment.

Philosophers also asked: what *justifies* cutting down all the trees from their hillsides, or sucking up all the water in the aquifers, or otherwise taking more from the Earth than the Earth can replenish? And is that justification sound? From Lynn White Jr's analysis of Christian dominionism and the Western obsession with technological progress,[28] to Arne Naess and the eight Platform Principles of Deep Ecology,[29] to John McMurtry and the analysis of the Value Program,[30] philosophers found that the roots of our ecological crisis lay in a faulty world view. To summarize it: people simply *believed* that they had the right to take what they wanted, without regard for nature's own needs. They held that belief for a variety of reasons. Some thought God had given us the Earth for the taking. Some thought human beings were somehow superior to all other forms of life. Some thought economic growth, with its demand for ever-increasing resource extraction, was the only way to lift the poor out of poverty. Some thought economic growth was an end in itself. All of these beliefs, so the philosophers claimed, were too *anthropocentric*, too much centred on the human point of view. We had to learn to see things from an *ecocentric* point of view. Paul Taylor, a major voice for ecocentrism in the 1980s and 90s, said that all environmental thought must be grounded in "a total rejection of the idea that human beings are superior to other living things"; this claim is "the most important as far as taking the attitude of respect for nature is concerned."[31] Francoise d'Eaubonne in 1974, and Karen J. Warren and Vandana Shiva in 1990, taught that patriarchy is also part of the anthropocentric view. As they saw it, the oppression of women and the domination of the environment follows the same logical structure and the same substantive value program.

These were some of the bold and forthright ideas in the air from the very beginning of the environmentalist movement in most Western countries. They were serious, action-oriented, pervasive, and even optimistic, although the latter quality was perhaps not obvious at first. Speaking personally: these ideas configured the vocabulary of most spiritual people I knew during my formative years. Most of them felt their sense of oneness with the Earth so deeply and profoundly, that they were convinced the greening of the self, and then of the world, was inevitable.

Nor were these ideas all theory and no practice. In fact, they produced at least two practical principles which some politicians and some corporations did, at least for a while, adopt in their policies. The first was the principle of Sustainable Development, proposed by the authors of a UN-commissioned report in 1987. The report defined the principle as "development that meets the needs of the present without compromising the ability of future generations to meet their own needs".[32] The second was the Precautionary Principle, proposed by Hans Jonas.[33] The most common version of the principle runs like this: "When an activity raises threats of harm to human health or the environment, precautionary measures should be taken even if some cause and effect relationships are not fully established scientifically."[34] By the turn of the millennium, the idea of the Green Self and these two practical guides for high-level policy seemed to form a global consensus about how all humanity could respond to the climate crisis.

It's been nearly seventy years since the first proclamation of "the greening of the self" (well, according to that little list). *Yet all the major indicators of planetary biosphere health continue to decline.* Species extinction rates continue to rise. Biodiversity continues to decline. Deforestation and desertification increases. Temperatures rise. Storms are more destructive and more frequent. The acidification of the ocean progresses. Floating garbage patches in the oceans grow. More and more people die from air pollution and heat waves. The problem is not that the idea of the Green Self lacked logical coherence or explanatory power. Nor is it that it couldn't be translated into political action, or into artistic and spiritual inspiration. Rather, the problem has to do with the practical and observable fact that despite more than half a century of promoting the Green Self in schools and universities, in films and television, in government and corporate policy, and the like, nonetheless the climate crisis carried on. *The greening of the self did not happen.* The argument can be expressed in a straightforward *modus tollens*, as follows:

1) If people adopt an ecocentric world view, then they will do what needs to be done to abate the climate crisis.
2) People did not do (enough of) what needs to be done to abate the crisis.
3) Therefore, people did not adopt an ecocentric world view.[35]

Premise 1, as you can see, is the basic proposition advanced by Schweitzer, Leopold, Naess, Warren, Shiva, and virtually all the important progenitors of contemporary environmental philosophy. Premise 2 is the measurable result expected to follow from the 'inevitable' expansion of the moral sphere and the adoption of the Green Self. The self did, perhaps, go green among people who are already disposed to it. Perhaps you are one of them. But it has certainly *not* occurred among the majority of wealthy and powerful parties who are in any kind of position to stop the climate crisis on a global scale.

I suspect the Green Self didn't catch on because its first requirement, to reject the idea that human beings stand superior to all other life on Earth, produces too much cognitive dissonance. We already tacitly accept the idea that some human beings are superior to other human beings, in terms of entitlement to wealth, fame, and power. Some people openly reject the view that all human beings are equal in rights and dignity; some assert the superiority of one (fictitious) race over others, or one gender over others. But let us leave aside for now the question of *why* it didn't happen. It's enough right now to observe *that* it didn't happen. And so the climate crisis carried on.

We could try new methods to influence people to adopt the Green Self. But I would like to consider whether we need a new big idea, a new way of thinking and seeing. What might that be?

Pure Anthropocentrism Didn't Work Either

The field of environmental philosophy provides some obvious answers to one of the root questions of philosophy: 'what, if anything, is intrinsically good?'. To make things simple, let's set aside, for the moment, any discussion about how landscapes may have intrinsic value, or how animals and plants might have rights, or how an expanded concept of the self could include our surrounding landscapes and ecologies. Let's look at only the answers that come from a purely utilitarian, purely human-centred view, of environmental ethics.

It should be obvious that clean air to breathe, and clean water for drinking, cleaning, and cooking, are instrumental goods. *Life* is the intrinsic good. I'm following philosopher John McMurtry's conception of 'objective good' here, in which something is good insofar as deprivation of that thing leads to loss of life-capacities for thinking, feeling, and acting, up to and including loss of life itself.[36] There might be more things to go on that list, but I'm keeping it simple for now. Given that definition, we can draw the conclusions that:

1) An ecology and biome surrounding one's community, of sufficient richness and stability and biodiversity to provide a reliable supply of clean air and water, is an objective good. They are necessary for our continued possession of life. Without them, we are all dead.

2) A system of economics and politics which regulates the community's extractions-from and impacts-upon those ecologies and biomes, to keep them within local and global carrying capacities, is, at the very least, an instrumental good.

Conclusions like those might be enough to motivate us to face the crisis. But our politics and economics, and indeed our culture, on the whole, behaves as if people believe a functioning biome is merely a nice thing to have, and that no serious consequences follow from harming it. Why do people believe that? It is not simply, nor only, that people think human beings are superior to the rest of life on Earth. For it is likely that most people don't think much about the rest of life on Earth, most of the time. Rather, it is that people believe there will always be enough air and water, and that ecologies and biomes can always bear the loss of whatever we take from them, and always carry the load of whatever waste or pollution we send back to them.

But as anyone who has studied ecology will know, *that belief is false.* That belief, which I shall call *the illusion of infinite carrying capacity*, was not seriously examined or doubted in the whole history of urban civilization until the rise of mathematical ecology in the mid nineteenth century. Plenty of people today, perhaps yourself among them, understand that the Earth's carrying capacity is limited. But plenty more people behave as if they believe it is infinite. Or, perhaps more accurately, they behave as if they don't think about the Earth at all. So it is not a matter of feeling superior. Rather, it is a matter of willed ignorance. *Pure anthropocentric reasoning does not take the circle of life seriously enough.* Were it to do so, it would soon cross a threshold after which it is no longer pure anthropocentric reasoning. Hence, it has also failed, so far, to deliver a solution to the climate crisis.

And God Is Not Coming To Save Us

Many people believe that they don't have to care about global warming and the climate crisis because they expect to be saved by God.[37] For example: Tim Walberg, a conservative politician from Michigan, told his constituents at a public meeting in 2017:

> "I believe there's been climate change since the beginning of time. I believe there are cycles. Do I think man has some impact? Yeah, of course. Can man change the entire universe? No. Why do I believe that? As a Christian, I believe that there is a creator in God who is much bigger than us. And I'm confident that, if there's a real problem, he can take care of it."[38]

Let's call this view *theological quietism* – the view that we need do nothing about the climate crisis; we need only live pious lives and wait for God to do the rest. Christian leaders including Pope Francis,[39] Orthodox Ecumenical Patriarch Bartholomew,[40] and two different Archbishops of Canterbury,[41] have rejected this view. But it remains widespread. It is one of the reasons why some politicians resist efforts to reduce greenhouse gas emissions, or resist regulations on pollution and waste. If God is coming to save us, then we need only wait for him; we waste time, and postpone His arrival, if we try to save ourselves. Indeed, some Christians believe that we should want the condition of the world to grow worse, in order to accelerate the return of the

Messiah.[42] Such is the broad concept I'm considering here.

There are some obvious objections to it. For instance, there might be no God. Or, theological quietism improperly denies our (God-given) human agency and freedom. Or, there are other conceptions of God which show that God gave the Earth to us as a responsibility. Perhaps we are the stewards of the Earth, not the owners, and we are in some sense commanded to take care of it. Or, seeing as there are plenty of calamities in history where God did not intervene to save anyone, it is therefore reasonable to suppose God might not save us from this one either. Or, there might be many gods, not just one, and therefore all the presuppositions of monotheism are wrong. Perhaps the gods are not in the salvation business: perhaps they relate to us in other ways.

But let us take theological quietism at face value. Then we should ask: what must you do to *deserve* God's saving intervention? You must "follow justice and justice alone, so that you may live and possess the land the Lord your God is giving you." (Deuteronomy 16:20).[43] The most important moral teachings of Abrahamic monotheism concern justice. We are called upon to "loose the chains of injustice... share your food with the hungry, and to provide the poor wanderer with shelter..." (Isaiah 58:6-8), to regard "whatever you did for one of the least of these brothers and sisters of mine, you did for [God]" (Matt 25:40), and to avoid the cardinal sin of pride: "Those who behave arrogantly on the earth in defiance of right – them will I turn away from My signs..." (*The Holy Quran*, 7:146). If the climate crisis is left to continue, and the powerful and influential of this world decide to do nothing and wait for God to clean up the mess: such people will have forged the chains of injustice, withheld food from the hungry (who starve due to droughts and crop failures caused by the climate crisis), abandoned the poor wanderers (who today include climate refugees escaping famine and desertification), treated the least of God's brothers and sisters with contempt, and behaved arrogantly on the earth in defiance of right. Those who preach the virtues of doing nothing in the face of calamitous preventable human suffering have already had their reward. They're not getting another one, in this life or the next. Theological Quietism thus descends into hubris.

Some might think I've cherry-picked the scriptures to suit my purposes. After all, the same scriptures also say, "Do not store up for yourselves treasures on Earth... but store up for yourself treasures in Heaven" (Matt 6:19-20). In other words, we should gamble our lives (and everyone else's lives) on the chance that life on Earth is worthless compared to life in the hereafter. I suppose it's possible that the God of monotheism exists, and that he could save the world as soon as tomorrow. However, seeing as no one may know when that might happen (1 Thessalonians 5:2), we should not plan for it. And we would be foolish, if not also sinful, to assume that anything we do would either accelerate or postpone it. Perhaps God will reward those who help individual people who have been harmed by the climate crisis. But that is not as good as preventing the crisis in the first place, as far as you are in a position to do so. Ah, but that requires us not to wait! That requires us to change the world!

What Is The Circle Of Life?

The climate crisis is not a normal kind of problem. It's not like a larger-scale version of a leaky bathtub or a broken furnace. *It is the kind of problem which calls for a new way of thinking about the world.* The Green Self was one such new way of thinking. In these meditations I shall search for another. But to create new ways of thinking about the world, we must first pose new questions, so to arrange what we know into new orders and new revelations.

Let's begin with a straightforward and mostly factual kind of question: *What is the circle of life?*

You probably remember the answer you were taught when you were a child. The circle of life is the food chain, or as most ecologists call it now, the food *web.* It's the system by which solar energy enters the biosphere of the earth, gets taken up by plants, microbes, and heat-retaining materials like water vapor and greenhouse gases. The microbes build up the soil, the plants eat the soil, the herbivores eat the plants, the carnivores eat the herbivores, and the apex predators eat the carnivores as well as some of the herbivores. So, the energy of the sun, having been transformed by primary producers into various sugars, proteins, and lipids, makes its way up to the top of the food web. Then it returns to the bottom of the web when the apex predators die, and their bodies feed the scavengers, the detritivores, and the microbiome of the soil. The microbiome feeds the plants, which get eaten by the herbivores, and so the energy cycles back into the system.

You might have learned that the food web overlaps with several biogeochemical cycles. For instance, there's the water cycle, in which sunlight causes water to evaporate from lakes, rivers, and oceans, form into clouds, travel, and fall again as rain or other precipitation. There are *two* different carbon cycles. In one, carbon dioxide is taken up by plants, turned into oxygen, and released into the atmosphere, where it is breathed by animals, turned back into carbon dioxide, and released again. In the second, carbon dioxide is released into the atmosphere by volcanic eruptions, dissolved into water when it rains, deposited on the ocean floor, and returned to the mantle as the Earth's tectonic plates subduct under each other. From there it can burst forth again in another volcano: a cycle taking millions of years to complete. There are similar cycles for phosphorus, methane, and oxygen: the basic chemical elements of life.

This version of the Circle of Life is elegant, useful, and clear. It's also simple enough that it can be explained to small children. "Everything you see exists in a delicate balance," says Mufasa to his son Simba, in the Disney film *The Lion King* (1994). "When we die our bodies become grass, and the antelope eat the grass. So we are all connected in the great circle of life."[44] There is nothing wrong with that conception of the Circle. Yet if predator-action and decomposition were the only forces driving it, then the predators should have eaten everything in their paths billions of years ago, and then died of starvation, leaving only the detritivores to inherit the Earth. If parasitism was the main driving force, the circle would grind to a halt as soon as the parasites run out of new hosts to attack. Clearly this has not happened: the earth proliferates with life in abundance. So, something else is going on.

The simplistic version of the Circle of Life also has another aporia. If life takes up energy from the sun, then where does all that energy *go*? If life only moves that energy around the ecosystem, shuttling it from one organism to another without releasing it back into space, surely the surface of our planet should be as boiling-hot as an oven. Yet that, too, has not happened. For most of her history, Earth has tended to remain at a mostly-comfortable temperature for life.

Given these two paradoxes, there must be more to the Circle of Life than the simplistic version describes. If we had a better understanding of the Circle, we might solve these paradoxes. We might also understand why the Circle is broken, and what we can do about it.

In Nature, There Is No Balance Of Nature

I often find that historical perspectives help me to view hard questions in new ways. Even the most beautiful ideas do not descend from the sky, fully-formed and complete, like angels from a Platonic heaven. Ideas, no less than people, have lives of their own. So let's explore the history of science for a while. Where did the idea of the circle of life come from?

Ecology, as a modern science, begins with German botanists, among them Ernst Haeckel (1834-1919) who coined the word *ecology* itself. Haeckel defined it as "scientific natural history": something familiar enough to people of his day, although as the discipline adopted a more mathematical disposition a new definition had to be found. From about the mid-1960s and onward, ecology gained a new definition as the science "concerned with species populations as members of communities inhabiting a certain abiotic background in which there maybe competition or cooperation."[45] But this is only one definition among many, and ecologists continue to wrangle about it, even to this day.

Ecology's first big idea is the famous "balance of nature": the idea that the interdependence of all life on earth produces an imprecise yet nonetheless reliable equilibrium, a general stability in population size and geo-spacial distribution, and a general preservation of the character of landscapes as forests, as grasslands, as deserts, etc. The first appearance of this idea in print (in the history of science, anyway) came in 1721, from the natural historian Richard Bradley (1688-1732), as follows:

All bodies have some Dependence upon one another; and

that every distinct Part of Nature's works is necessary for the Support of the rest; and that if any one was wanting all the rest must consequently be out of Order... We observe so Exact a Harmony between Natural and Mathematical proportions, as might give every thinking Man Reason to believe the latter could not have been without the former; or that the laws or rules of Mathematicks, as they now are, could not be just, if Nature's laws were different from what we now observe them to be.[46]

While other naturalists of the time thought their business was to identify and catalogue new species of living things, Bradley studied how living things interact with each other. He also looked for further predictions and conclusions that could be drawn from the study of the interactions. For instance, in the winter of 1728-9, he observed that a population of moles had buried themselves (for hibernation?) a foot deeper in the soil than usual. He theorized they were chasing the worms, and that the worms had gone deeper because they somehow "knew" the coming winter would be more severe than usual because of "their structure and tender disposition". In such a manner, he thought he could predict the weather. He was wrong, but only for lack of information, not for being stupid.

Two years after first publishing his ideas, Bradley was appointed professor of botany at Cambridge, though without salary, which suited him fine as he cared more about writing books than teaching students. In that position, the idea of the balance of nature gained more academic prestige and influence. In 1887 botanist Stephen Alfred Forbes (1844-1930) published *The Lake As A Microcosm*,[47] an essay now regarded as one of the founding documents of the science because of its more precise treatment of the balance of nature concept. As he defined it, the balance of nature "holds each species within the limits of a uniform average number, year after year, although every one is always doing its best to break across its boundaries, on every side."[48] How does that balance happen? Forbes explains:

It is a self-evident proposition that a species cannot maintain itself continuously, year after year, unless its birth-rate at least equals its death-rate. If it is preyed upon by another species, it must produce regularly an excess of individuals for destruction, or else it must certainly dwindle and disappear. On the other hand, the dependent species evidently must not appropriate, on an average, any more than the surplus and excess of individuals upon which it preys, for if it does so, it will regularly diminish its own food supply, and thus indirectly, but surely, exterminate itself. The interests of both parties will therefore be best served by an adjustment of their respective rates of multiplication, such that the species devoured shall furnish an excess of numbers to supply the wants of the devourer, and that the latter shall confine its appropriations to the excess thus furnished. We thus see that there is really a *close community of interest* between these two seemingly deadly foes.[49]

Forbes also saw that this balance of nature preserves itself using violence. His closing paragraph, which emphasizes that violence, is worth quoting at length:

In this lake, where competitions are fierce and continuous beyond any parallel in the worst periods of human history; where they take hold not on the goods of life, merely, but always upon life itself; were mercy and charity and sympathy and magnanimity and all the virtues are utterly unknown; where robbery and murder and the deadly tyranny of strength over weakness are the unvarying rule; where what we call wrong-doing is always triumphant, and what we call goodness would be immediately fatal to its possessor, – even here, out of these hard conditions, an order has been evolved which is the best conceivable without a total change in the conditions themselves; an equilibrium has been reached and is steadily maintained that actually accomplishes for all the parties involved the greatest good which the circumstances will at all permit. In a system where life is the universal good, but the destruction of life the well nigh universal occupation, an order has spontaneously risen which constantly tends to maintain life at the highest limit, – a limit far higher, in fact, with respect to both quality and quantity, than would be possible in the absence of this destructive conflict. Is there not, in this reflection, solid ground for a belief in the final beneficence of the laws of organic nature? If the system of life is such that a harmonious balance of conflicting interests has been reached where every element is either hostile or indifferent to every other, may we not trust much to the outcome where, as in human affairs, the spontaneous adjustments of nature are aided by intelligent effort, by sympathy, and by self-sacrifice?[50]

What strikes me most about the work of Bradley and Forbes is their use of the vocabulary of *ethics* to describe something that they believed was a *natural* phenomenon: they speak of the balance of nature as a system of harmony, support, goodness, order, beneficence, and self-sacrifice. By using the language of ethics, the concept of the balance of nature becomes not simply a system of organic processes to be studied objectively. Right from its very inception, the concept appears as a system of moral values, in the sense that it evaluates natural phenomena for their apparent moral character.

Furthermore, the concept also presents itself as an *inversion* of ethics. Forbes is explicit about it. He says 'what we call wrong-doing is always triumphant'; virtues like mercy and charity are 'utterly unknown'; vices like robbery and murder and tyranny 'are the unvarying rule'. These values are contrary to every foundational moral teaching provided by every religion in the Abrahamic tradition, and contrary to most secular systems of ethics in Western philosophy up to that time (with the possible exception of Machiavellianism). Yet Forbes upholds this moral inversion as both a natural fact as well as an instrumental moral good: "where every element is either hostile or indifferent to every other", he says, "there comes about a harmonious balance". To be fair, Forbes adds the caveat that human intelligence, sympathy, and self-sacrifice can also help to preserve the balance. This softens the inversion of values. But it also reinforces that the concept of 'balance' is an *ethical* system: it treats nature as a field of moral evaluations.

The balance of nature is a system of ethics for another reason: it evaluates natural phenomena for their applicability to human society. Another essay by Forbes states that we human beings, and *only* we humans, interfere with the balance:

> There is a general consent that primeval nature, as in the uninhabited forest or the untilled plain, presents a settled harmony of interaction among organic groups which is in strong contrast with the many serious maladjustments of plants and animals found in countries occupied by man.[51]

That statement may appear to contradict other statements he made in *The Lake as a Microcosm*. Yet it, too, reinforces the idea that the balance of nature is a system of ethics. As far as the history of science is concerned, the 'balance of nature' has always been a system of ethics, and among the first few generations of ecologists there were no exceptions.

Indeed, the idea was so popular at the time that some philosophers used it to create a new version of the Design Argument for the existence of God. In 1802, for instance, English philosopher William Paley published the now-famous

"Watchmaker Analogy". It goes like this. If you happened to find a pocket-watch lying on a beach, its complexity and the smooth functioning of its inter-related parts would tell you it was deliberately designed by a watchmaker, even if you had never seen a pocket-watch before. Similarly, according to Paley, the balance of nature displays the same kind of complexity and smooth functioning, and therefore tells you there must have been a designer. Here are his own words:

> Every indicator of contrivance, every manifestation of design, which existed in the watch, exists in the works of nature; with the difference, on the side of nature, of being greater and more, and that in a degree which exceeds all computation. I mean that the contrivances of nature surpass the contrivances of art, in the complexity, subtilty, and curiosity of the mechanism; and still more, if possible, do they go beyond them in number and variety; yet in a multitude of cases, are not less evidently mechanical, not less evidently contrivances, not less evidently accommodated to their end, or suited to their office, than are the most perfect productions of human ingenuity.[52]

By the end of the 19th century, arguments like these made concept of the balance of nature a core doctrine of ecology, and indeed of theology.

But scientists looked closer, and found that humanity is *not* the only force that can disturb nature's balances. A wetland, over a span of decades, can become a grassland, and a grassland can become a forest, all without human intervention. Today this principle is called *ecological succession*. It was introduced into science by Frederick Edward Clements (1874-1945), who described it as follows: "Each stage reacts upon the habitat in such a way as to produce physical conditions more or less unfavourable to its permanence, but advantageous to the next stage."[53] Clements also thought that there's a small number of end-state outcomes, which he called climaxes: "Grassland or forest is the usual terminus of a succession." (*ibid.*) At that time, ecologists had not yet come up with the idea of an *ecosystem*, but Clements was getting there: at the very least, he was accounting for the observable fact that all ecosystems are perpetually changing their populations, their communities, their overall character.

The implication is that in the world of nature, insofar as science has been able to determine, there is no such thing as 'the balance of nature'. No ecosystem ever remains itself, so to speak, having the same community of organisms, the same ratio of predators to prey numbers, the same volumes and flow-rates of water and oxygen and other materials. Predator and prey populations do rise and fall with each other, but there is no stable oscillation between them, either in terms of absolute numbers or in terms of ratios or relative population densities. Charles Sutherland Elton, for instance, wrote in 1930 that: "'The balance of nature' does not exist, and perhaps never has existed. The numbers of wild animals are constantly varying to a greater or less extent, and the variations are usually irregular in period and always irregular in amplitude."[54] And while the principle of succession is well established and evidenced now, nonetheless there is no evidence for stable climaxes. Instead, there are many possible climax states for virtually all types of ecosystems. Some of them are cyclic, going back and forth between two or more climax states, and some succession processes stop before arriving at the predicted climax. In general, an ecosystem could be considered close to climax when its biodiversity is very high. But nothing in nature ever remains stable, consistent over time, in harmony, and in balance. Ecosystems are chaotic and unpredictable. Not even the controlled and pristine environments of computer-simulated ecosystems show us balance and harmony in its community of virtual life.

And yet – and yet – when I go into the Gatineau Hills park, which I like to think of as 'my' forest, everything *looks* like it's in balance. I see the same creatures today as I did ten years ago when I first came to live on the park's edge. I see the same birds in their seasons every year, the same trilliums in the spring, the same colours on the trees in autumn. The coyotes have not eaten all the deer, nor have the deer moved away and starved the coyotes. There's a tallgrass meadow in the park a few kilometres from my home which, over those years, has been colonized by broadleaf hardwood trees. Soon the meadow will be a woodland, and soon after that, a forest. But when that transition is complete, it will look much like the rest of the park's forest. And so it shall join into a new harmony. Perhaps anyone whose experience is similar to mine will think that since the forest community doesn't much change, that therefore its life is balanced, and its members live in harmony. And indeed this apparent harmony is good for me. It's beautiful to look at. And we all depend on it for the oxygen we breathe, the water we drink, the food we eat. My friends and I used to sing songs of gratitude and of spiritual participation in the balance. Those were happy times in my life.

But I have to remind myself that my view is limited. If I counted only what I could see with my own eyes, I would miss things. I have seen a few effects of the climate crisis in my forest, but there are places in the world where the crisis is coming faster, and with more destructive effects. For example, in the village of Lytton, British Columbia, on 29th June of 2021, the temperature reached 49.6°C. Wildfires forced the people of Lytton to evacuate. In the days that followed, most of their homes were destroyed.[55] In August 2021, the town of Floridia, on the Italian island of Sicily, endured an entire week of temperatures in the high 40s, including a spike on 13th August when the air soared to 51°C. Snails cooked to death in their shells. Oranges and grapes melted off the trees. A farm worker told a journalist: "All of us who work in this sector, in agriculture, understand it... And we are the base of everything. When you take the broad view, Europe is dying."[56]

When it's that hot, no amount of drinking liquids and sweating can save you from organ failure. And even if your house, your public transit, your workplace, your car, and your shopping centre has air conditioning, the machines cannot dehumidify the air enough to cool you down. When it's that hot, they stop working.

In order to understand how a forest which looks harmonious and balanced may actually be in a state of crisis, I need instruments that allow me to see what lies beyond the horizon of my own point of view. Travellers' tales, archives and libraries, media communications (insofar as they are trustworthy), science, philosophy, and reason, are among those instruments. There may be more. We shall have to use them all, to figure out the best answers to the root questions.

For the absence of balance in nature *is not the reason the circle of life is broken*. To find out how and why it is broken, we need to look closer.

Twelve Paths to Ecology

Ecology is, among other things, the study of life as a global complex system. Life is a *system* in the sense that it involves multiple elements and parts, each having their own properties and behaviours, existing in various necessary and inalienable relationships to other elements and parts. Life is *complex* in the sense that the sum of all the interactions in the system can produce new properties, some belonging to the system as a whole and not to any individual member of the system: properties whose nature cannot be predicted by analyzing the parts individually. And life is *global*, in that life-systems with emergent properties have now taken over the whole of the Earth. Life has been found in the most inhospitable and unexpected places on Earth, such as deep-sea thermal vents, acid lakes, the sea floor beneath 900 meters of Antarctic ice,[57] and down to five kilometres beneath the surface of the Earth.[58]

I'd like to meditate on the second of the three concepts noted here: complexity. In science, a complex system is a system with *emergent properties*; that is, properties of system as a whole which cannot be predicted from knowledge of the individual parts of the system. Michael Polyani, a chemist and philosopher who mentored several students on to Nobel Prizes, set the stage for this way of thinking in the 1960s by arguing that organic life is an emergent property of nature: organisms cannot be entirely reduced to the physics and the chemistry that underlies them.[59] A good example of this can be seen in the flocks of birds. Geese, robins, buzzards, and flamingos flock together in V-shaped patterns to take advantage of the 'wake' in the air created by the leading birds, and thereby stay aloft with less energy. Starlings and sandpipers *murmurate*: they gather in large flocks of thousands of animals, and together they take off and land, move, change direction, change shape, and avoid predators as if the flock was a single organism, with a single mind. Mathematicians and computer scientists have studied the phenomenon, and found that it can be modelled with a small number of simple rules:

1)   Stay close but not too close to the other birds.
2)   Move in the same direction as most of the nearest seven birds are moving.
3)   Move away from predators.

I remember as a boy watching starlings migrate in long rivers across the sky: millions of birds, taking all afternoon to pass over the house where I grew up. I have not seen that sight now in some thirty years or more.

Nor are bird murmurations the only examples. Fish, dolphins, bats, and ants follow broadly similar rules when they move together in large numbers. So do the root tips of plants, as they grow into the soil, seeking the optimal distribution. Slime-moulds, colonies of millions of single-celled organisms moving together, can solve maze puzzles, reproduce the layout of a subway network on a model of a city, and select the healthiest food from a diversified offering, without needing a central nervous system or a brain.[60] Clouds of fireflies, when enough of them have gathered together, wink their lights in near-unison with one another, giving the impression that the light is a wave travelling from an origin-point somewhere in the cloud, and spreading out from there. The rule is simple: each firefly tries to flash its light in less and less time after the moment when another nearby firefly flashed its light. The fireflies don't have to watch thousands of other fireflies that way, and they don't need centralized coordination; they need only watch the nearest half-dozen or so. Muscle cells in animal hearts follow a similar rule: contract as soon as you feel the nearest neighbouring muscle cells contracting. Similar rules govern the construction of termite mounds, so that the mounds keep a consistent internal temperature and the air circulates to remain breathable, again without centralized planning or design.[61]

Examples like these, I think, underscore the beauty of complex systems and their emergent properties. The rules are simple, and each member of the system follows them mostly autonomously, and yet the system as a whole, considered separately from its constituent parts, self-organizes into persistent structures with unpredictable, emergent properties.

Do ecosystems as a whole have emergent properties? I think that they do, and in this meditation, I shall present you with my summary of the rules that produce them.[62] I shall resist calling them laws, since some of them have local exceptions. But they are true more often than not, and useful for grasping how things work in the world of nature. I shall call them *paths*, so that we may compare them to the courses followed by rivers, or the tracks made by forest creatures. They never remain for long in the same exact vector, but also never stray far from the same general direction or the same general destination.

So here we go:

1 - All living things reveal themselves, emerge into presence, come into visibility.
The unfolding of flowers, the emerging of plants from beneath soils or from beneath winter snow, the birth of animal offspring, climbing out of burrows and nests, caterpillars transform into butterflies, the moon waxes, the sun rises. And this may seem like a Heideggerian point, however not all revelations are of *aletheia*, 'truth'; for some things reveal themselves in camouflage. Chameleon lizards and cuttle fish can change their colours, for example. But even that is a kind of revealing: things are revealed in their disguises, their performances, their appearances.

2 - All things respond to events around them.
Animals perk their heads when they hear strange sounds. Prey animals like the deer bound away when a predator emerges from the tree line. Birds sing out the dawn chorus. Plants turn their leaves to face the sun. Even the tiny microbes investigate the objects and particles that they bump into, assessing them for whether they can be eaten. Each life's emergence into presence also opens the possibility that another life may take notice and respond.

3 - All living things follow cycles, repetitions, and rhythms.
Patterns in the leaves of trees, symmetry in the shape of flowers and animal bodies, reproduction of offspring who in turn produce similar offspring after the morphology of the species, the flashing of fireflies in the night, the beating of animal hearts, walking and running, waking and sleeping, hibernating and migrating in their seasons.

4 - All living things change themselves.
Though repetition is an observable fact, no repetition is exactly

the same as the next. Each iteration of a form, shape, size, mode of behaviour, etc., introduces something new into the music, even if that newness is subtle, non-obvious, evident only after careful and close inspection. This is one of the bases of evolution and natural selection: and another way in which living things reveal themselves.

5 - All living things dwell in a niche, a settlement; all things belong somewhere.
Fish remain in the water, amphibians prefer shorelines. Some kinds of plants prefer arid soils, others prefer moist soils. Some need hot climates; others need it colder. Some creatures explore their geography to find a niche, others create one by building nests or damming streams.

6 - All living things explore beyond their niche.
Driven by curiosity, opportunism, and by hunger and other forms of necessity, bees search for new flowers, goats climb rocky cliffs in search of new grazing, farm cattle break their enclosures and enter new pastures (I've seen this happen), predators expand their hunting territory, prey creatures search for better hiding places. Plants release seeds into the air, climb walls or cover the nearby ground, and push roots deep into the earth. All things constantly test the boundaries of their niche, so to expand the niche or discover new ones.

7 - All living things compete.
Predators kill and eat their prey; plants outpace other plants for soils and waters and sunlight; breeding-age animals select their mating partners and chase their rivals away.

8 - All living things cooperate.
Animal mothers nurse their young; trees use subterranean fungi networks to share nutrients and information about insect

attacks or changing seasons; pack hunters strategize to ambush a prey; some primates trade food for sex and for grooming services. Between this principle and its predecessor, we could draw some analogies to the old Greek sage Empedocles who said all things are caught between Love and Strife. There are some non-obvious forms of cooperation too, such as resource partitioning: life forms which hunt the same foods divide their hunting areas into zones, so that they won't directly compete with each other.

9 - All living things pass on what they gather.

Gathering, of course, means consuming food. It also means assembling materials to make things like bird's nests, termite mounds, and beaver dams. After the gathering, the birds pass their nests to their offspring; beavers bequeath their ponds and channels to fish and other wetland creatures; oxygen and carbon and food and water is passed on to others through breath and urine and excrement; everything a life-form gathers into its body and holds there passes back to the world through death and decomposition.

10 - All living things change the world around them.

This is, of course, a straightforward consequence of the previous path. Life changes the distribution of things, their chemical composition, their availability to other organisms. Between this path and its predecessor, it is clear that nothing released into an ecosystem ever vanishes or goes nowhere. Minerals, gases, fertilizer chemicals, pollution, sewage, litter, and heat: all of it comes to a landing where it could be gathered by life, changed by life, and passed on by life, for the benefit or the detriment of life. Combining this path to ecology with the previous three, we can understand the deep structure of the popular ecological motto "everything is connected".

11 - *All living things die.*

This observation is perhaps the final implication of all the previous paths. Each organism must someday cease to gather, as the telomeres on their DNA erode to nothing and so cell-replication takes on too many errors. Or as injury or disease or depravation leaves it unable to move. Once it can no longer gather, it must melt into the realm of the unseen, like a fire out of fuel, a candle at the end of its wick.

12 - *Life goes on.*

Organisms die but ecosystems carry on; indeed they carry on in part precisely because organisms die, and in dying pass on what they have gathered. Ecosystems are in theory immortal, so long as their energy sources remains constant, the biogeochemical cycles function, the frequency of intermittent disturbances remains low, and the lives lost to death can be replaced by new births or by migrations from one ecosystem to another. There is no such thing as balance in nature, as we have seen. Yet ecosystems can persist beyond the time-scales of civilizations, thus giving an impression of immortality. They can do this by following the same rules as individual organisms: following patterns, changing themselves, gathering and passing things on.

In your own exploring of the World of Earth, you might discover more paths than these. You may also discover an exception or two.[63] But these twelve discoveries are enough for the current purpose.

The vast diversity of life on Earth is one of the emergent properties that follows from them. Each organism passes on the genes it gathered from its parents, and makes slight changes to them on the way. When the changes in their genes give an advantage in the course of exploring new niches, then over time the community may branch itself from its origins, resettle in a new niche, and become a new species.

In the next meditations, I will explore additional emergent properties for ecosystems that I think follow from these paths: the primacy of symbiosis, and the persistence of dissipative structures. By exploring them, we may find resolutions for the two aporias in the simplistic version of the Circle of Life. And though it may seem unscientific, we may also discover a kind of love.

The Primacy of Symbiosis

In earlier meditations, we saw that the simplistic version of the Circle of Life has too many problems. We also saw that the notion of 'the Balance of Nature' doesn't exist in nature; that nature is in fact chaotic and unpredictable. All this, and we are barely getting started!

And yet – nature somehow produces order out of the chaos. Forbes, in *The Lake as a Microcosm*, saw that nature, continuously involved in "destructive conflict", nonetheless somehow produces "an order... which constantly tends to maintain life." And even though nothing in nature comes to balance, as Forbes thought, nonetheless organic life has, indeed, taken hold of this planet and held it for some 4.6 billion years, including through five mass extinction events and five major ice ages. If there was not at least something resembling 'balance' in the simplistic version of the Circle of Life, if there was not at least some orderliness in nature, life would surely have extinguished itself millennia ago.

So, how is it that life possessed our planet so successfully? How is it that "life finds a way"?[64] The answer to that question might be the complete version of the Circle of Life that we are looking for.

Ecology is, among other things, the science of relationships in the natural world. The simplistic version of the Circle of Life described only two kinds of relationship: a predator eating its prey, and a dead organism fertilizing the soil. But this is not enough to explain the long-term persistence and the astonishing diversity of the natural world. By my count, the Circle of Life has not two but *six* types of relationships, as follows:

1. *Predation*: one organism kills another for food.
2. *Parasitism*: one organism, the parasite, takes things from another organism, the host, without killing it. But the host suffers a loss of life-functioning, possibly leading in the long run to its death.
3. *Commensalism*: one organism takes things from a host organism, but the host loses none of its life-capacities; indeed the host might not notice the other organism at all.
4. *Facultative symbiosis*, also called *mutualism*: two organisms trading things for mutual benefit, although both are able to live and thrive without each other if necessary.
5. *Obligate symbiosis:* two organisms trading things for mutual benefit, and without this relationship they die.
6. *Symbiogenesis*: two organisms whose obligate symbiosis has grown so close that they now reproduce together as if they were a single organism.

Of these six relationships, the three varieties of *symbiosis* are the most significant. This may not seem obvious. The simplistic version of the Circle of Life presupposes a worldview in which individualism, struggle, competition, violence, and survival-at-any-cost dominates all relationships. We saw this already in Forbes' *Lake as a Microcosm*. It also appears in most versions of the theory of evolution. Early adopters of the theory such as Herbert Spencer and Thomas Malthus, both of them economists and not biologists (Malthus was also an Anglican priest), thought that Darwin's theories proved that all animals, including human beings, are naturally disposed to aggression. The famous phrase that nature is "red in tooth and claw" comes from Spencer, not Darwin.[65] This worldview found additional validation in

Garret Hardin's famous 1968 essay *The Tragedy of the Commons*, in which he argued that all cooperation is self-defeating. And in 1976 Richard Dawkins gave us *The Selfish Gene*, of the most influential scientific books of all time, in which he argued that the genes which survive natural selection are the ones which, pedagogically speaking, serve their interest in self-replication. Guided by this worldview, it's hard to see how symbiosis might be favoured by natural selection. Indeed, under this worldview, it's hard to see how symbiosis exists in the world at all.

But it does. Examples are easy to find:

- Some species of ants have learned to 'farm' aphids: the aphids get protection from predators, and the ants drink the aphid's sugar-rich excretions.
- Birds and fruit bats eat the fruit from trees, gaining food, and in return the trees get their seeds dispersed over more territory when excreted with the animal's poop. The animal droppings also provide nutrients and moisture for the seeds.
- Egyptian plovers clean the teeth of crocodiles for food: the crocodiles, in return, get better dental health.
- Remora fish clean the teeth of sharks, for the same mutual benefits.
- The clownfish makes its home inside the body of sea anemones: the clownfish attracts predators which the anemones paralyze, and then both creatures gain their food.
- Lichens, once thought to be a distinct kind of plant, are a symbiotic pairing between fungus and algae. The algae provides food for the fungus, and in return the fungus provides a structure for the algae and protects the algae from dehydration.
- The Whistling Thorn tree, a type of acacia that grows on the Serengeti plain, has nodules on its branches which

provide food and shelter for ants. In exchange, the ants protect the trees from being grazed by giraffes and other herbivores.

- The Honeyguide, a bird that lives mostly in Africa, searches its habitat for beehives. When it finds one, it uses its song to invite local humans to break the hive open so both can enjoy the honey. Some Indigenous peoples in its habitat have learned to use a song to attract them; the bird then leads the honey hunters to a nearby beehive.[66]

- When ravens spot a sickly or wounded animal, they will sometimes draw local wolves to it with their loud and distinctive calls. The wolves then kill it, and both enjoy their dinner together. The two species have also been recorded playing friendly games with each other. Ravens sometimes tease the wolves by pulling on their tails, or picking up sticks to play tug-of-war with wolf puppies.[67]

- The human stomach and intestines are home to a variety of microbes which are not genetically human, and which help break down complex molecules in our food. They get the sustenance they need; in return, we get a more efficient digestive system.

Most of those examples are behavioural. Symbiosis also occurs at the level of cells and genetics. In the 1960s, molecular biologist Lynn Margulis, for example, found evidence that that evolution itself began through the merger of bacteria to form multi-cellular organisms. She also found evidence that the mitochondria in animal cells are the descendants of parasites which attacked us billions of years ago, but which survived the deaths of their hosts by evolving into obligate symbiotes. From these discoveries Margulis posed the theory that symbiosis, not predation and not parasitism, is the stronger force in evolution, on both the global and the cellular perspective. "The tendency of 'independent' life," she wrote in *The Symbiotic Planet* (1998) "is to bind together and re-emerge into a new wholeness at a higher, larger level of organization."[68]

In the late 1990s, Canadian forest ecologist Suzanne Simard found that Douglas Fir and Paper Birch trees transfer carbon to each other through a vast underground network of mycelia (mushrooms and fungus). Investigating further, she found that not only firs and birches, but all the trees, and all the shrubs and grasses, are connected to the mycelial network in the soil. Competition is still involved: some plants use the network to steal carbon from other plants, or to inhibit the growth of other plant species. But Simard also discovered that trees transmit *chemically-encoded information* through this network: chemical signals that warn other trees about dangers such as insect attacks or a deficiency of nutrients. Further, she discovered that forests have Mother Trees: older trees in the network which respond to those signals by sending nutrients to help vulnerable trees to grow. Through them the forest becomes, in effect, a kind of super-organism; and without them the forest is less able to survive dangers like fires, pest invasions, or clear-cut logging. Trees also use the mycelial network to 'eavesdrop' on each other to learn of successful defence strategies. Without this network, forests would have less biodiversity, less resilience, and less longevity.[69]

Although it may seem a stretch to call it symbiosis, apex predators can have a mutually beneficial relationship with organisms who interact with their prey. While a predator takes the lives of its prey, the consequences of the predation can bring life to many other species. A prime example of this is the re-introduction of wolves into Yellowstone National Park, in 1995, after an absence of seventy years. In that time, the deer grazed most of the ground-covering plants away, leaving large areas of the park nearly barren. When the park authorities brought in a pack of wolves from Alberta Canada, they killed some of the elk and the deer, as you might expect. The surviving elk, in turn, moved to areas of the park where it was harder for the wolves to hunt them. The ground cover returned to the over-grazed areas. And then the trees returned: in only six years, the trees grew five times higher. The return of the trees allowed songbirds to return, as well as animals that use trees and tall grasses for shelter, such as rabbits, beavers, and mice. The beavers built dams and ponds, creating habitats for muskrats, amphibians, and fish. Then the bears returned, attracted by the berries on the trees. They, like the wolves, helped keep the elk population down, with similar effect on the plants and trees. The strengthened trees also helped the soils along riverbanks to resist erosion, stabilizing their banks.[70] In ecology, this phenomenon is called a *trophic cascade:* it's what happens when the actions of creatures near the top of a food web ripple down through the system, affecting everything below, potentially including the physical geography of the land. They're like long chains of cause-and-effect connecting top predators with everything else in the ecosystem. Each step in the chain might be any of the six aforementioned kinds of ecological relationships. But the overall net result of a trophic cascade tends to be beneficial for the whole ecosystem. It's possible for a trophic cascade to have a detrimental effect on the system, but the majority of the research says that they tend to create benefits: they help ecosystems keep biodiversity high, they improve the cycling of nutrients, they limit the populations of mid-level predators, and they provide sustenance for scavengers.[71]

The point of this meditation is to say that symbiosis solves the paradox of how the Circle of Life has carried on for millennia despite the self-destructive logic of predation and parasitism. The three varieties of symbiosis, and the long-range symbiosis of the trophic cascade, taken together as forces of cooperation, are stronger than competition and predation. This can be hard to see if we look at the Earth as an aggregate of individuals competing for resources and survival. Margulis, Simard, and other ecologists are teaching us to see the earth as a complex system in which everything is directly or indirectly involved in all the life around it, and in which symbiosis and cooperation, across multiple levels, keeps the system as a whole flourishing.

So here's a first preliminary answer to the first root question: What is the circle of life? *A complex system of organic inter-dependence and inter-relation, in which many different kinds of relationships obtain, the most influential of which is cooperation.*

Little Whirlpools

The simplistic version of the Circle of Life had a second aporia: if energy enters an ecosystem from the sun, where does it go? We can find out by looking at the physics of energy in open systems.

The biosphere of the Earth is a large thermodynamically open system, and the Sun is its energy source. As energy flows into the system, the system pushes back, so to speak, to radiate that energy out again. Push more energy into the system, and the system radiates it out again at a higher temperature.[72] Push too much energy in, perhaps beyond the system's *tipping points*, and the system changes its state: it finds new pathways for the radiation of its energy, or it breaks down altogether. So, the short version of the answer to that second aporia is that the energy of the Sun which hits the Earth gets radiated back into space, mostly in the form of infrared light. But how does the Earth do that? Let's look a little closer.

Around the year 1824, the mathematician Joseph Fourier wondered why the Earth was so warm. Following some simple calculations, he figured that if the Earth was in thermal equilibrium with the energy it received from the sun, its average temperature should be minus-18°C. But the Earth's average temperature back then was +15°C, a difference of 33 Celsius degrees. His discovery led to what we now know as the Greenhouse Effect. You've probably heard of this effect before. Solar energy gets captured by the surface of the Earth and also by the atmosphere. Lower levels of the atmosphere re-radiate the energy out and down to the surface again, trapping heat in the biosphere. Higher levels of the atmosphere re-radiate the energy back out to space. The transition between those layers takes place at an altitude that depends on the whole atmosphere's average temperature. That temperature, in turn, depends on the atmospheric concentration of heat-retaining substances like water vapour, methane, and carbon dioxide.

Fifteen degrees Celsius also happens to be a comfortable average temperature for life. This led the scientist and inventor James Lovelock, more than a hundred years later, to wonder whether that was not a coincidence. It also happened that Lovelock was employed at the time by NASA to help design instruments that could detect life on Mars. He theorised that if life was present on a planet, we could detect it remotely by analysing the chemical makeup of its atmosphere. In much the same way that cells in animals and plants use internally circulating streams of nutrient-delivery and waste-elimination, such as blood, life forms of an integrated ecosystem would use the oceans and the atmosphere as the medium for the exchange of organic compounds.

From these axioms Lovelock and his collaborators, Lynn Margulis among them, produced the Gaia Hypothesis, or as most scientists now call it, Earth System Science. The idea may be summarized in three basic concepts:

1) The evolution of life and of the physical elements always occur together.
2) The earth as a whole behaves as though it is a single organism.
3) Life on the global scale acts in such a way as to create and maintain the conditions most favourable to life.

As a whole, the biosphere of the Earth has feedback processes which control the temperature, the oxygen and carbon dioxide content of the atmosphere, the salinity and pH balance of the oceans, and other factors, to keep them at a state that's comfortable for life. In Lovelock's words:

The Gaia Hypothesis said that the temperature, oxidation state, acidity, and certain aspects of the rocks and waters are at any time kept constant, and that this homeostasis is maintained by active feedback processes operated automatically and unconsciously by the biota...[73]

So there's the short version of the solution to the second aporia of the Circle of Life. The energy that an ecosystem captures from the sun gets radiated back to outer space, mostly in the form of infrared light, while at the same time feedback processes in the biosphere (i.e., the Gaia system) trap enough heat to keep the biosphere comfortable for life.

There's a word for that heat-dissipation effect: *entropy.* The second law of thermodynamics, which governs entropy, was discovered by Nicolas Carnot in 1824 and Rudolf Clausius in 1850, in experiments conducted on steam engines. They found that not all of the heat in the boiler was transferred into forward motion: some of that heat was wasted. And it was not possible to build an engine that didn't waste at least *some* amount of heat, however small. Thus arose the classical definition of entropy: the tendency of energy in closed systems to degrade to a state that is unavailable to do work. Entropy applies not only to heat-gradient systems like steam engines. It applies to any system in which energy of any kind is transferred from one place to another to do work, including the energy that powers the growth and locomotion of living things.

But living organisms seem to defy that law. Life persists, life remains, life goes on. Organisms synthesize highly ordered molecules in their cells, like sugars and lipids, using the disordered morass of energy around them in sunlight, soils, the biomass of their food, and atmospheric gases. These molecules serve as the energy-units of organic systems which, like the Earth itself, preserve their equilibrium by capturing, holding, and dissipating a more-or-less constant flow of energy.

Knowing this, it is perhaps helpful to think of a living organism not as an object, nor even as an individual 'being', but instead as a *dissipative structure,* like little whirlpools or tornadoes. It exists only as long as matter and energy flows around it and through it; indeed, it exists only as a local perturbation in a general flow of energy through its environment. A dissipative structure is never in a state of equilibrium with its surroundings: it is never 'balanced'. But it persists over time by preserving the pathways by which energy flows through it and around it, and also by modifying those pathways in order to resist disturbances and find new stabilities.[74] Dissipative structures produce order from disorder because they have the wonderful property of being *self-organizing.* Canadian biophysicists Eric Schneider and James Kay explained how this works:

> ...dissipative structures self-organise through fluctuations, small instabilities which lead to irreversible bifurcations and new stable system states. Thus the future states of such systems are stable over a finite range of conditions and are sensitive to fluxes and flows from outside the system... these thermodynamic relationships are best represented by coupled nonlinear relationships, i.e. autocatalytic positive feedback cycles, many of which lead to stable macroscopic structures which exist away from the equilibrium state.[75]

This suggests that self-organising processes, such as ocean currents, atmospheric circulation, and DNA replication, are an effective means of dissipating energy. Or to put it another way, in which the full meaning of this principle will be clearer: *life exists on Earth because of entropy – life emerged on Earth as a means of dissipating the energy of the sun.* As Schneider and Kay put it,

> ...living systems are dynamic dissipative systems with encoded memories, the gene with its DNA, that allow the dissipative processes to continue without having to restart the dissipative process via stochastic events. Living systems are sophisticated mini-tornadoes, with a memory (its DNA) whose Aristotelian 'final cause' may be the second law of thermodynamics.[76]

An Aristotelian Final Cause, by the way, is the *reason* why something exists. It is the *telos,* the purpose or the goal, to which something aims in everything it does. Schneider and Kay are not the only scientists to suggest that ecosystems might have a final cause. Stuart Kauffman, theoretical biologist, theologian, and philosopher, argued that the *telos* (the aim, end, or purpose) of all complex systems, from quantum dynamics to the biosphere, is to self-organize to increase the range of 'the adjacent possible', that is, to increase the number of events that could happen next after any thermodynamic work cycle.[77] Admittedly, the idea that the biosphere has a final cause is speculative, and might be too theological for some scientists. But it has some interesting explanatory power. It explains, for example, why there is so much biodiversity on the Earth. The more organisms there are in a given ecosystem, and the more types of organisms (ie. species) there are, then the more pathways there are for the ecosystem to dissipate energy. With more pathways, the ecosystem is not only more efficient: it is also more resilient. It is better able to resist or assimilate the effects of a disturbance, and so carry on fulfilling its *telos*, dissipating energy.[78]

And with that, we have a more complete solution to the aporia, and another answer to our first root question. What is the Circle of Life? *A self-organizing, dynamic energy-dissipation system; a system of organic inter-relation and inter-dependency which, while never in a state of perfect balance, maintains itself by dissipating energy (as its* telos), *and by increasing its biodiversity (as the* techne *serving the* telos.)

Tipping Points

In the last meditation I mentioned the concept of the *tipping point*. A simple way to explain it is like this. If you bent the wire of a coat hanger or a paper clip by only a small angle, it would bend itself back to its original shape. That's like the system absorbing the energy-input from your fingers and expelling it out again, to preserve itself in its current stable state. If you bend it beyond a critical angle, it bends into a new shape.[79] That's like the system finding a new stability which accounts for the input of energy. Another example: if you tipped a coffee-cup on its side to only a small angle, it will settle back in place when you take your finger away. But if you tip it too far, it falls to its side.

All the extra carbon dioxide that our industries have pushed into the atmosphere and the ocean – thirty-six billion tons per year, or about four hundred gigatonnes since the Industrial Revolution, or about two-thirds as much CO_2 as existed in the biosphere over the previous million years[80] – is like bending the coat hanger wire, or tipping a coffee cup. Push it only a little, and the system absorbs the energy or pushes back against it. Push it too much, and something somewhere might bend into a new shape, or fall down. Since the global biosphere is a system of inter-relation and inter-dependency, when one part of it bends into a new shape there can be consequences for other parts, which themselves have consequences for other parts, and so on, resulting in a drastic change in the shape of everything. The point beyond which those kinds of system-wide drastic changes become inevitable is called a *tipping point*.

All complex systems have tipping points. Consider as an example: the Atlantic Meridional Overturning Circulation, better known as the Gulf Stream, the ocean current which keeps

Europe warm. Cold water in the North Atlantic is denser than warm water, so it sinks. This creates a kind of 'negative pressure' zone, or a kind of suction force, which pulls in surface water to replace it. That surface water comes up from the Caribbean, which is warmer. The cold water that sank flows south along the ocean floor, and is pulled up to the surface again when it reaches the Antarctic Circumpolar Current. By the time it gets there, it has mixed with warmer water in the equatorial and temperate regions, so it's warmer than the meltwater coming from Antarctic glaciers. So it rises, and goes into the Indian and Pacific oceans where it helps contribute to the annual monsoon rains. Eventually it makes its way back to the Caribbean. The Gulf Stream is thus only one part of a single closed-loop circuit of water that wraps around the entire planet. This circuit is called Thermohaline Circulation, better known as the Global Conveyer Belt, and it takes about five hundred years for a given drop of water to travel the whole length of the circuit.

Now imagine what would happen to this system if some part of it is disturbed: say, if global heating causes more ice in Greenland to melt into the North Atlantic. The meltwater is less dense than ocean water because it's fresh and not salty. So it doesn't sink. So there is less 'negative pressure' to pull warm water up from the Caribbean. So, the Gulf Stream slows down. Then Europe cools down. The heat in the Caribbean water stays where it is, where it helps to warm up the lower levels of the atmosphere. This extra heat-energy causes winds to blow harder, which causes more tropical storms. Meanwhile, other areas of the conveyer belt also slow down. That causes other parts of the world cool down or heat up, changing rainfall patterns in those regions. People who depend on those rains for their agriculture get a drought or a famine. Many of them die. Some of those who survive choose to leave: they walk the earth as environmental refugees, changing the political situations in the places where they arrive, and in the places they leave behind. Complex systems, complex relationships, complex consequences.

Alas, I am sorry to say, this situation is not hypothetical. The tipping point for the Gulf Stream is already almost reached.[81] There are nearly a dozen other tipping points like it in the global biosphere: the disintegration of the Greenland ice sheet, the shift of Russia's boreal forest, the die-off of the coral reefs of Indonesia and Australia, a shift in the African and Indian monsoon rains, and a dieback of the Amazon rainforest following deforestation, as examples. Nor are the political consequences of crossed tipping point only hypothetical. Several consecutive years of drought in Syria, for instance, as well as in nearby countries that Syria depends on for most of its grain imports, were a major cause of the ongoing civil war that followed the Arab Spring.[82]

It's not that the Circle stops turning altogether after a tipping point is crossed. Rather, the Circle searches for new stable states, new stable pathways for the dissipation of entropy. Resilience, not efficiency, is the important principle here. Systems will resist or assimilate a disturbance for as long as it can, but a powerful and sudden disturbance can force the system to change its state. The period between the departure from the former state and the settling into a new state can be violent and unpredictable: a danger to related ecosystems, and a danger to the rest of the Circle.

There is no gentle or easy way to say this: As the climate crisis proceeds, the final stability that the global Circle of Life settles upon is likely to make large territories of the Earth, possibly whole continents, unsurvivable for humans, and indeed unsurvivable for the great majority of life on Earth as we find it today.

So let us consider a third answer to my first root question. What is the Circle of Life? *A system of organic interdependence, as per the previous answers, which is subject to disruption and unpredictable transformation should one or more of its members disturb the functioning of its pathways beyond the system's ability to adapt.*

The circle is moving toward a new stability with less biodiversity, less biomass, fewer symbiotic relations, and in general less life, *even though the deep function of the Circle is to increase those metrics of life* as part of its energy-dissipation system. This is part of why I say that the circle is damaged, struggling, suffering: or to put it viscerally, *broken.*

And perhaps calling to us for help? But that possibility calls for another meditation.

Love

Those last three meditations had rather a lot of analytic and scientific argumentation, didn't they? And at their end, although I am confident in my conclusions, still I wonder if I was losing the forest for the trees. Perhaps it's a good time to remind myself why I wanted to learn ecology and philosophy in the first place.

In my life, there has always been a forest. As a child, there was the Barber Scout Camp, south of Guelph Ontario, where my Dad sometimes brought his students for a week of nature education and my Mom and sisters and I joined him in the evenings. We also camped in Cyprus Lake, in the Bruce Peninsula, for a week every year. It's where I learned the names of the trees, how to handle a canoe, how to use a fishing rod, how to climb cliffs, how to avoid rattlesnakes and wasps, and what poison ivy looks like. On the cliffs overlooking Georgian Bay, with the far shore invisible over the horizon, I learned how to think about infinity. In adolescence, there was a house my grandfather built for his retirement, near Ayton: it sat in the centre of thirty acres of maple bush, where my siblings and cousins and I learned how to be free. Then there was the Elora Gorge Conservation Area, which I began exploring when my family moved to the village a week before my ninth birthday. In my early adulthood, there was the Arboretum at the University of Guelph, and the campgrounds that hosted WiccanFest. In my grad school years, there was the Vogelsberg of Hessen, where a thunderstorm taught me of the

Immensity. And there was the wild Atlantic coast of Connemara, the cliffs and monuments of Aran Island, and the fields around Kells and the Hill of Tara. Ireland is my father's country: he was born there, and taught me some of its stories. I made his country my own for a while: I explored its passage-mounds and stone circles like a modern-day Druid looking for The Morrígan. Sometimes, I thought I found her.

Today, in my middle years, I spent several summers in meadows and woods and hills of central Bohemia, Czech Republic, where I wrote three books. And I have the Gatineau Hills Park, in west Quebec, which begins across the road from my home and carries on into La Peche and La Chase, and into imagination. In different times and for different reasons I have loved all of these forests. Apart from my home and its library, the forest is the place where I feel most like myself, where I feel most at peace. The thought of living without one causes me grief. Perhaps you, too, prefer green fields and blue skies over the machinery and clatter of the human world. Perhaps that is one reason why you took up these meditations with me.

I rejected the Christian Doctrine of Original Sin when I was sixteen. In my late twenties I rejected the Laws of Magic: the 'Law of Attraction' is nothing more than observer bias supported by peer pressure. Yet whenever I visit the forest, I remember why animism is such a persistent, elemental experience. I feel welcomed in my forest. I feel understood, and cared for. The feeling often starts when I come across a grove or a corner where all things suddenly become timeless, as though somehow new and freshly alive while also ancient and enduring. Sunlight becomes otherworldly, as it filters through the canopy and trembles with the trembling leaves. From there, the feeling grows into the sense that I am being watched, that I am not alone: a feeling that can sometimes be uncomfortable, and yet which also turns a country walk into a pilgrim's journey. It reminds me to speak softly, and to speak only of the highest and deepest things. Some places give me the feeling that the land knows who I am. Others give me the feeling that I ought to stay, and never return to civilization. The feeling arises more easily when I find a perch on the rock stacks, or a window in the tree-line, where the Immensity fills my entire field of view. Looking at the dome of the stars from the top of a hill, the meadow in which I sit suddenly becomes the centre of the universe. All the trees around me become a congregation, doing homage to the celestial glory.

But on most occasions the experience is simple, and not even unusual. I might come around the corner of a trail and find a rabbit. We regard each other. It is like a conversation. Of course, part of the exchange stems from the fact that the rabbit is a prey animal, and he wants to know whether I'm going to chase him. But another part of me sees the rabbit as the face of the forest, showing part of itself to me, and acknowledging me. It's like a "check-in": the soul of the forest wants only to remind me that she is there. And I go into the forest to remind her that I'm here, too. It is a brief and silent conversation; but it is good and beautiful enough. Nothing more needs to be said.

Animism, as the simple proposition that the things of the natural world are in some hard-to-express manner alive and spiritually present, seems to offer itself despite all objections. I might scientifically understand everything there is to understand about a flower – its biology, its niche in the ecosystem, the structure of its cells, the chemistry of its life-processes, its symbolism in various arts and cultures – and yet the feeling of its spirit seems never to disappear. What if there's something more to this flower? What might that 'something more' be? And could it inspire the work needed to heal the Circle of Life?

The beauty of the forest, its spiritual presence, and a deep love for it, should be enough by itself to move people to protect the forest. But I also know that not everyone feels this kind of spiritual presence. Not everyone had a forest in their life since their childhood; and not everyone who did have a forest grew to love it. Some people who do feel a sense of the spiritual nonetheless do not find it in forests. Perhaps they find it elsewhere: in churches, in rock concerts and raves, in religious writings, or in works of art. And many people, on finding visible evidence even in their own neighbourhoods that the local ecology is breaking down, feel no remorse. Indeed, these are further reasons why the greening of the self didn't happen. At least, not in the West.

The Dialogue of the Seen and the Unseen

It is time to change questions. Time to take up a different kind of thinking. Now that I know, at least analytically, what the Circle of Life is, perhaps I can now examine it as a *phenomenon*: a feature of the world that you and I live in, a presence in our lived experience, a revelation of values and meanings to which we respond in various ways, or fail to respond.

To examine the Circle of Life in a new way, I must set aside, as far as I can, the Things Of Men.[83] To do this, I must first move my body out of the village, away from the Things Of Men, and sit myself in a place where I can contemplate the World of Earth with the fewest possible distractions. On top of this hill, in the middle of my forest, the engine noises from cars on the roads are muffled, and the houses are mostly hidden behind the trees of the valley. I still see a few Things of Men nearby: a hunter's platform, the dog's electronic collar, and the machine-manufactured clothes on my body. The hills themselves have been sculpted into their present shapes by thousands of years of farming. But I've found a place where there are no houses, no roads, no long-distance power lines. They're all hidden behind the hills. In my field of view there is only meadow, and its flowers; only trees, and the gentle waves of breeze rolling through their leaves; only the good blue sky; only the good green Earth.

Having stepped away from the Things of Men, it's easier to set aside the presuppositions and interests that arise from my involvement in the Things of Men. My hope is that by setting such things aside, it will be easier to see the Earth: its reality, its value, its meaning. Fortunately, I already know how to do this. There's a field among the Things of Men for which we have powerful and complicated feelings, similar to our feelings about the metaphysical and the divine: that is, our feelings about *art*. We use some of the same words for good art as we do for scenes of earthly wonder: we say they are beautiful, sublime, magical, eye-catching, awe-inspiring; we relish them, we enjoy them, we are uplifted by them. This is only a *prima facie* point, but I think it is enough to suggest an argument-by-analogy, as follows: perhaps I can escape the consciousness engendered by the Things of Man in the same way that I escape the consciousness of the everyday when I contemplate a work of art. That is to say, I could adopt what philosophers call *the aesthetic attitude*. In philosophical history, this goes back at least as far as Shaftsbury, Kant, and Hume, who wrote that artistic appreciation involves 'disinterestedness', that is, the suspension of an interest in personal gain or loss in relation to what you are looking at. So, here on this hill, I must tell myself that I am not here to gather firewood, or to hunt any animals, or harvest crops, or in any way to mix my labour with the land in order to produce anything. I shall also suspend my intention to take a holiday, or to take exercise, or to walk this dog. By suspending all these ways of thinking, I can appreciate the World of Earth for its own sake, and then perhaps the answers to my questions will find me.

Life in the World of Earth, as I've described it in my Twelve Paths, appears to us in ways that also suggest, or hint at, further things or events not (yet) revealed. For example, the way a creature responds to events is itself an event to which other creatures may respond. The dawn chorus of the birds alerts other birds, and awakens the sleeping rabbits and field mice in their underground burrows, and other creatures further on. It becomes a chain of call and response, which 'turns the corner', so to speak, leading over the hill or around the river bend, and so out of sight.

The realm of the unseen is not transcendental, nor supernatural: it is *imaginal*. Things are unseen because they are hidden. But they are also in some way expected. The unseen is *that which is hinted and promised by the seen*. It is like the contents of a gift-wrapped package a moment before it is opened, or the silence in the concert hall a moment before the conductor begins the performance.

A dialogue opens in my mind: a conversation between the empirically observed and the logically or conceptually inferred, the tangible and the intangible, the perceived and the imagined,[84] or to sum it up, *the seen and the unseen*. By ancient tradition, metaphysics is the branch of philosophy that studies the real; here I shall take it to mean the study of the dialogue between the seen and the unseen which leads to the configuring of the real. Notwithstanding Kirikin-tha's First law of Metaphysics, "nothing unreal exists,"[85] the really interesting metaphysics questions are the ones about the unseen: questions about infinity, totality, freedom, the gods, the self, the soul, the origin and the destiny of the world. In the example of the dawn chorus, the realm of the unseen is that which is hidden from me by space and time. As already observed, creatures and whole landscapes change themselves from one generation to the next: it is impossible to know in advance exactly what will be changed, impossible to know how things will be different. Before each new variation is revealed, it lies hidden, but imagined, in the realm of the unseen. Now, when those changes emerge to the realm of the seen, we might find they are only a repetition, in the main: the differences from the previous repetition might be insignificant, barely noticeable. But that too can be imagined and expected, and the fulfillment of the expectation can be pleasurable. The winter might have been long and harsh, and therefore the return of spring, familiar and expectable and absolutely unsurprising, nonetheless awakens feelings of comfort and relief, a sense that things are as they ought to be.

Food webs, chemical cycles, and other functions of the Circle of Life, also involve a turning of the corner, where some part of the cycle moves things out of sight. Oxygen is recycled into carbon dioxide by my lungs; that same unit of carbon dioxide is carried off by the breeze and recycled into oxygen by an oak tree somewhere behind me, possibly many miles away. From this discovery that certain organic cycles pass through the realm of the unseen to find completion, we can easily imagine that while those materials are out of sight, they might spread out anywhere, all over the earth, helping any number of creatures on the way.

Any of these inklings from the realm of the unseen can be enough to fill a heart with spiritual delight. But the promise of the unseen can expand further still, to include nothing less than the whole earth. My breath goes on to join the entire atmosphere; the water I drink comes to me from clouds born over faraway oceans. And so we might conclude 'we are all one'. And while I think that conclusion is too pat and simplistic, nonetheless there is a feeling, or a kind of rational imagining, prompted by the behaviour of life in the realm of the seen, which suggests that when things turn round the corner they can go anywhere and be everywhere. They can transform into any-*thing,* too. And they can re-enter the realm of the seen at any time, from any direction.

Why does any of this matter? Contemplating the whole earth as a mystery box about to be opened, a curtain about to be drawn back, a dark room about to be illuminated: it is precisely this same revealing-action which we also love in other forms of art. Especially narrative storytelling. What we love about science fiction and fantasy, for example, is the threshold, and its promise of transport to another world: through a blue police box, or an attic wardrobe, or down a rabbit hole, or out the nursery window and into the sky. An exploration of a landscape offers the same sense of a threshold, and of other worlds beyond. What is on the other side of that hill? What is through that hollow hedgerow? What dwells 'beyond the ninth wave', that is, the horizon of the ocean? The answer may be broadly predictable:

another valley, another tall grass meadow, another island. Broadly predictable, but never *precisely* predictable; it is always possible to encounter the unexpected. A new species of animal or tree. A new geography: the timbre line at the edge of the taiga, or an oasis in the desert. You might object that this is not as impressive as a tornado blowing your house into the Land of Oz, and therefore the analogy is weak. But it is the natural revelation which inspires (and is exaggerated by) the fictional; it's not the fictional which inspires (the interpretation of) the natural. We humans have been exploring the World of Earth since long before we put our stories into writing. And when we did start writing stories, some of them were about what might dwell in the realm of the unseen. Otherworld journeys, starring heroes like Anaeus, Inanna, Orpheus, Scarface, Oisin, and Horus. Odysseus' journey home, and the fantastic monsters encountered on the way. Gilgamesh's quest to reach the gods and to demand an explanation for why we die. From these stories and their ritual re-enactments are born religion: or to be more precise, the kind of religion which is an attempted communication with whatever might dwell in the realm of the unseen. Maybe the history of religion is a history of how the hidden-but-promised became (spoken of as) the transcendental? But I digress.

Another criticism: it might be more objective to say the World of Earth simply *is*; the trees and soils and stones exist in their here-ness and now-ness but they do not otherwise say anything. So, if I say that a dark cloud promises rain, that says something about my state of mind, and not about the cloud. In that sense, the World of Earth does not hint at the unseen. It is I who so hints it, but I pretend otherwise to myself.

A reply: yet the World of Earth is arranged and constituted in a way that this sense of hinting-at-the-unseen is a logically fitting response to the seen. There is at least one feature of the visible world which fits especially well: the *threshold*. I've mentioned some kinds of thresholds already: hill crests and river bends.

There's also animal dens, the depths of deep waters, the hearts of dense forests, and the sphere of the stars above. And, it is worth noting, the places where the threshold appears to fill an exceptionally wide span of your field of view, such as mountain heights, or star fields unobstructed by light pollution, are the places where people tend to describe the feeling of spiritual revelation dawning upon them *unbidden*. The best examples are the spiritual experiences described by atheists. People who have decided the gods don't exist still often encounter the oceanic feeling, the sense of awe, and the uncanny, which some psychologists (including Sigmund Freud) regard as the emotional foundation of religion. This suggests that there is something in those larger thresholds, or perhaps more accurately there's something in the special combination of those thresholds and the open state of mind which encounters them, which carries the realm of the unseen into reality.

There should be nothing especially strange about the idea of visual thresholds inspiring aesthetic experiences. It's rather like seeing a house that's painted yellow on the front, and imagining that the back is painted yellow, too. It's only when I'm *prevented* from walking around to the back of the house to see its colour for myself, that I might imagine its colour could be different, or even that the house is actually an enormous mansion, or actually a hollow facade. By analogy, then, it's only when prevented from knowing the unseen, that I might imagine that things which disappear into it are carried on to the infinite. In the World of Earth we are, indeed, so prevented. For however much of the earth I can see from this perch, I can never see all of it at once. However much of it I explore in my lifetime, I cannot explore it all. I don't have enough time before I die. I can expand the size of my niche, but I cannot break out of it. There is always a threshold: always a boundary between the known and the unknown. It scurries ahead of me wherever I run toward it; the slow rider who cannot be overtaken. And therefore, however much of the world I explore, there's *always* the possibility of nearby new worlds not yet explored. If I were to climb to outer space and see the whole earth all at once, I will have crossed one threshold only to encounter another: the stars, which hint at the planets that orbit them, as well as yet more stars too distant to be seen.

What I think this objection really points to, is not simply that I might be mistaken about who or what is doing the hinting about the unseen. It's also that however many of the Things of Man I leave behind, there's one Thing Of Man I cannot leave behind no matter what I do: *myself*. I can climb this hill and at the same time suspend the search for 'resources' like building materials or food; I cannot suspend that it is I who has climbed this hill.

When I am not searching for anything in particular, I find myself searching for the thresholds, for something-I-know-not-what. I'll search for anything, even the fantastic, because I can't give up the searching. (I'm seeing spectres of Sartre's judgment of human life: we are all "condemned to be free".) Thus I discover that there's a part of me which the World of Earth can bring out of the realm of the hidden-within-myself, and into the light: it's the part of me which imagines, and which loves to imagine; it's the part of me which loves the things-of-earth that prompt the imagination.

All Things Become The Things Of Man

The realm of the unseen, as the realm of the hidden-yet-promised, is not necessarily a realm of safety. This tall grass meadow might be home to dangerous animals like snakes and wild boar, disease-bearing insects like tics, poisonous plants and mushrooms that I might mistake for something safe to eat. The breeze which at this moment appears to promise gentle rain might instead bring a thundercloud. Danger can be a source of beauty. But here on this hilltop I am manifestly not safe. My dog and I are the tallest objects for at least one hundred meters in every direction: living lightning rods, if a storm should arise. It is also possible that while walking away, head in the clouds, I might step in a hole and break an ankle. The realm of the unseen, then, can be a source of wonder and fear simultaneously.

Further, the realm of the unseen is also an oubliette. For when we toss a tin can out a car window, when we leave the wrappings of our picnic lunch behind, when we flush anything down the toilet, or drop a bag of rubbish at curbside for the garbage workers to collect, it is precisely to the realm of the unseen that we consign it. Most people have no idea what happens to the things they throw away. Our waste products turn that corner, no less than the waters of a river, to be carried away in space and time.

But in the realm of the unseen things must follow the same paths as they do in the realm of the seen: for instance the path that says that all living things pass on what they gather. When things die their materials recycle, not vanish. Whatever we leave at the threshold will, imaginally, disperse around the world, and so, imaginally, return to us.

And herein dwells the connection to the climate crisis: it's a problem which appears to approach us from the realm of the unseen. When we consign our garbage and our pollution to the distance, we imagine that it gets cleaned up, assimilated, vanished away. Later, when we find that our summers are hotter, our winters shorter, our storms more numerous and more violent, and so on, it's our garbage and our pollution coming back to us. But we don't see it that way. Instead, we see these events as if emerging from behind a curtain, as if coming from around a corner. They look like just another way for nature to reveal herself. So the blame seems to belong to everyone and to no one.

Most do not see the complex web of relationships that lead from mass industrial carbon release, to global climate system instability. And most people *prefer* not to see them. We would rather hear the happier story about how nature takes care of us, and where we don't have to lift a finger to help it. We prefer the story that nature can handle it all, and that nature can always bounce back. We prefer the illusion of infinite carrying capacity.

I think this leads to another reason why the Circle of Life is broken: *the realm of the unseen*, no less than the physical surface of the Earth, *has been fully penetrated by humanity's industrial and consumerist powers.* And therefore, anything that appears to us as if emerging from the thresholds of the Earth could be, in some measure, a Thing Of Man.

Therein lies the insidiousness of the climate crisis. It looks like the natural order of the world even though it is, in fact, a product of human artifice. In that respect it is comparable to war, patriarchy, racism, capitalism, organized religion, and the state: things also designed by people, but whose effects also appear to follow from human nature. Contrary to the pronouncements of many prestigious philosophers throughout history, neither war nor the state nor patriarchy nor any of those human situations arise from nature. None of them are ordained by any gods or divine directives. None of them arise from fate or destiny. All of them are open to examination, criticism, abolition, and replacement. It is part of the function of civilization itself to persuade people that situations of human design are uncontestable features of revealed reality – this is the central problem with civilization, and the general foundation of the suffering and oppression it can cause.[86] But the climate crisis also differs from those other examples in at least this important respect. Racism, patriarchy, and so on, could conceivably be undermined by public protest, and other forms of responsible democratic action. But by contrast the climate crisis would carry on for decades even if every factory and power plant in the world closed today. That is the case because many of its chemical and material drivers – greenhouse gases, microplastic pollution, acidified ocean water, and so on – can remain in the global ecosystem for decades, where they can continue to drive the crisis.

We face *a collective consumer-industrial humanity as a global immensity.* It is subtle and soft in some places, and easy to miss. It roars like a monster in others, consuming all in its path. Though created and still driven by human actions, no single person or class of persons commands it. Like the fairy-tale sorcerer who summons a creature from the underworld that later escapes his control, the consequences of industrial consumerism are beyond any single person's ability to dispel. The climate crisis has infused itself into the Earth and into nearly all of the ecological relations that configure the human reality. This makes it almost impossible to avoid. It has no centre, and no boundaries. It is inside the air we breathe, the water we drink, the food we eat, the spaces we traverse, the world we perceive, the thoughts we think. Some people and some institutions are more responsible for it than others. But anyone can perpetuate it without a deliberate wish to do so. Indeed most of its contributors have no idea how they are contributing. It infects not only our bodies, like a disease. It infects our entire way of seeing, dwelling, thinking; our whole way of being in the world. Thus we face the possibility of a future in which *everything*, in some way, is a Thing Of Man, and nothing remains which belongs, wholly and completely, to the World of Earth.

Here we have another answer to this first root question: What is the Circle of Life? *A dynamic system of moving and transforming materials and energies, whose pathways flow over, and return again from, the horizon of the seen and the unseen.*

The Calling

Let's draw the answers to my first root question together. The Circle of Life is:

1) *A complex system of organic inter-dependence and inter-relation, in which the most influential relationship is cooperation.*

2) *A self-organizing, dynamic system of energy-dissipation.*

3) *A system which is subject to unpredictable transformation should one or more of its members disturb the functioning of its relationships beyond the system's ability to adapt.*

4) *A system where the lines of relation among its members flow across the horizon of the seen and the unseen.*

We can express the meaning of these answers together into a single proposition: *The circle of life is an immensity.*

That might sound flippant and simplistic. But the word 'immensity' has heavy significance in my philosophical world. I use it to name events and encounters in human experience with certain special qualities. They are unavoidable in life: they can sometimes be postponed or put off, but they always find a way into your field of view, whether you like it or not. They tend to stand above or beyond what an individual human mind can grasp in a single moment. They're not incomprehensible as such. But in the dialogue of the seen and the unseen, the Immensity always hints at further lengths and deeper depths: they approach as if from across a threshold of the unknown, suggesting that there is more to them than what has been revealed so far. They tend to impose their own meaning upon the situation in which they are encountered. You may think you know what's going on and you may think you're in charge, but the Immensity has a stake in the situation too, and it might be bigger than yours. The appearance of an immensity is a fundamental reality: something not manufactured nor glamorized, something not planned nor designed, something not controllable or subject to your will. Perhaps you can exercise some temporary and partial influence over it, but never for long: soon enough some new dimension appears, and it breaks free.

I draw my inspiration for this idea from an occasion in the summer of 2004, now many years ago but still large in my memory. While exploring the forests of Germany's Vogelsberg region with a friend, we were beset by a thunderstorm. The heavy winds and whipping branches reminded me – *forced* me to realize – that I am only a small thing in a great and ancient world that has existed for aeons before me and shall carry on for aeons after. Our worries for our safety in that moment, and later that day our exhilaration for having survived, was another immensity. The possibility that we might have died that day was a third. In the weeks that followed, I learned that other people had similar encounters in their lives, and similar feelings about them. I discovered versions of my big idea in the work of philosophers like Karl Jaspers and Emmanuel Levinas, and I was pleased to see that my 'big idea' already had a little bit of precedent. Certainly, a version of the call of the Immensity appears in the many nature writers who have described how the beauty and the wonder of the Earth moved them to love and care for the Earth, to want to protect it from industrialization and from pollution, and to want others to love and to protect the Earth, too. I'll spare you the big long list of names and books, except to say it was an eclectic mix of Hindu, Taoist, Indigenous, Irish, and neo-Pagan writers whose ideas churned about in my head like a kind of moving jigsaw puzzle.

In the year 2013, English philosopher Timothy Morton described the Circle of Life, and the climate crisis, as a *hyperobject* – a concept that seems similar to the Immensity, but requires a bit of explanation. As he defines it, hyperobjects are "things that are massively distributed in time and space relative to humans."[87] His examples include black holes in space, oil fields, mountain ranges, the solar system, and, intriguingly, "the very long-lasting product of direct human manufacture, such as Styrofoam or plastic bags, or the sum of all the whirring machinery of capitalism." They are viscous, in that they are "surfaces from which nothing can be peeled" and "we find ourselves caught in them".[88] They are nonlocal: a term he borrows from quantum physics to describe how hyperobjects can have more than one face, and appear in more than one place at the same time. And each of those faces are involved in "knotty relationships between gigantic and intimate scales". This leads him to conclude that "there is no such thing, at a deep level, as the local".[89] Hyperobjects involve timescales beyond the human: they're not infinite, but they offer very large finite timescales that are harder to cope with than infinity.[90] And finally, "they exhibit their effects *interobjectively*; that is, they can be detected in a space that consists of interrelationships between aesthetic properties of objects. The hyperobject is not a function of our knowledge. It's *hyper* relative to worms, lemons, as well as ultraviolet rays, and humans."[91]

In these meditations I will continue to use my concept of the Immensity. But I must acknowledge that Morton is on to something right. Both the Circle of Life, and the climate crisis, are bigger than any given individual event that instantiates them or takes part in them. Let me be bold and say: there is no field of human life that they don't touch. Take any example that you like, no matter how unrelated it might seem at first. In sports and athletics: higher heat and humidity poses a health threat to elite athletes competing in outdoor events. In financial services: over the last thirty years, the insurance industry has logged a large rise in claims for floods and fires. Properties in high-risk areas are increasingly classified as uninsurable. In race relations and the struggle for civil rights: urban neighbourhoods in America inhabited mostly by Black or Latino people have more air pollution, more water contamination, more flooding damage, and more fracking wells, than White neighbourhoods.[92] The list goes on.

The COVID-19 pandemic, for instance, could also be treated as a hyperobject. Its manifestation is not only the virus organism itself. It's also the way people fear it, and the way people deny it. It's the various prevention measures we've adopted, such as social distancing, wearing masks, washing hands; it's the strain on hospital resources, and the stress and despair of nurses and doctors and other medical professionals; it's the shortages of toilet paper and hand sanitizer during the initial outbreak; the ridiculous conspiracy theories about microchips in the vaccines; the class dimension in which poor people or Black people are statistically more likely to catch it and die of it because low-income housing and the precariat service economy make it harder to social-distance. It's the despair and grief of people whose loved ones died of it. Perhaps in the light of this example, the climate crisis is only one of many multi-dimensional, 'metaphysical' crises of our time.

Yet the COVID-19 pandemic is itself part of the larger immensity of the climate crisis. For as is now widely agreed by most public health researchers, the virus emerged as the climate crisis favoured the growth of the habitats where the disease-carrying animals live.[93] At the same time, deforestation, one of the causes of the climate crisis, destroyed the natural buffer-zones that once stood between us and those habitats.[94] There is also evidence that COVID-19 lay dormant all over the world, emerging when its habitat was right: strains of it were found in Barcelona sewage, in March 2019, months before the onset of pandemic in Wuhan, China.[95] New disease outbreaks caused by deforestation were predicted years in advance of the 2019-21 emergency.[96] Nor is the COVID-19 pandemic the only example. Fruit bats, attracted to areas which had been cleared for farming, and feeding on the insects that gather around electric lights, gave us the Ebola virus.[97] Malaria spreads when deforestation gives disease-bearing insects like mosquitos new habitats for breeding. HIV, the plague of the 20th century, entered human populations when poachers in sub-Saharan Africa ate meat from infected chimpanzees.[98] The climate crisis is like a many-tentacled monster whose fingerprints are themselves many-tentacled: pandemic diseases are one of its fingers.

There are other crises that may appear unrelated but which are, in fact, either caused by, or else multiplied and worsened by, the climate crisis. But I trust by now my point is clear. *The climate crisis itself is also an immensity*. It, too, is unavoidable and inescapable. It, too, is greater than any one person's ability to grasp or to understand; it may even be greater than the ability of whole nations to grasp and understand. It, too, is a fundamental reality, a *metaphysical* reality.

Now, it may seem just like an ivory-tower snob to say there's something metaphysical about a phenomenon that is killing or ruining the lives of millions of people around the world. In popular language, the adjective *metaphysical* points to something abstract, or fanciful, or belonging to a higher plane of existence, as we might say of the gods. But the storms, heat waves, droughts, floods, and the like, are certainly not metaphysical to the people whose lives have been ruined by them.

But the concept of Immensity also has an ethical dimension. Phenomenologically speaking, the immensity calls to you. Its presence requires a response. There can be many different ideas of what constitutes an ethical response to the Immensity, but there is no relativism here. The good life must always be lived in concert with the Immensity, the fundamental reality, and it's the immensity which sets the conditions for the possibilities of the good life. The choices that remain for individuals, as indeed for communities and nations, amount to experiments with different ways of being in the world which, in dialogue with the Immensity, do or do not result in a worthwhile life for the individual and her associates.[99]

The visible effects of the climate crisis are, if nothing else, signs or portents of a complex system in which something is going wrong. We tend to be more alert to disturbances and disruptions in the systems we live in, more so than we are alert to their harmonies. When the gears and ball bearings and other parts of our bicycles are working properly, we do not much think of them; we know when a musical instrument is out of tune even if we don't know how to tune it. In social situations, we often sense what is wrong before we know what is right; *in*justice elicits indignation before justice elicits praise. Thus the latest flood, the latest heat wave, the latest tropical hurricane, appears to us as a fault or a disruption in the world, even if we don't know much about how the biosphere is supposed to work, or what its proper functioning should look like. This knowledge, this sense of something-going-wrong, is like an ethical summons. We are called to find out exactly what has gone wrong, and why. And we are called to do something about it, if we can. Perhaps we are called to restore an original harmony, if we can figure out what that original harmony was like. Perhaps we are moved to create a new harmony, once we decide what kind of new harmony is desirable, or for that matter possible.

This sense of being-called, or being-summoned, is what I think might replace the notion of the Green Self. So far, we have learned *what* is calling to us. But to explore what new philosophical dimensions this sense of calling might reveal, we must move to the next root question: *Who* is called?

Second Root Question

Who Faces The Circle of Life?

People tend to frame their local or personal realities in terms of an encounter – a struggle, a dialogue, a confrontation, a romance, an exchange, a *facing* – with some principle of ultimate reality. Or, if not an ultimate reality, then they frame it in terms of a reality of a higher order than their own. For the poets of the ancient heroic ages of Europe, the authors of the *Táin Bo Cuailnge*, the *Sagas* and *Eddas*, the *Illiad, Beowulf*, and so on, the human reality finds itself in relation to fate and destiny, sometimes represented as the will of a chief god, sometimes as a force in its own right, and in any case irresistible and mostly unknowable. For theologians in the Abrahamic tradition, the human reality finds itself in relation to the God of monotheism; though to be fair, God is conceived in this tradition in many different ways. In Hinduism, we exist in relation to *Brahman* and *Samsara*. In Confucianism, we exist in relation to society, understood in terms of filial piety and the Five Relations. For existentialists like Jean-Paul Sartre and Simone de Beauvoir, and phenomenologists like Emmanuel Levinas, the human reality finds itself in relation to Others. That is, other people who are so unlike oneself that they cannot be defined as one's opposite. Nor can they be understood by comparing similarities and differences: they live by their own definitions. For Martin Heidegger, a philosopher who was influential, brilliant, obscure, and notorious, the human reality finds itself in relation to the unfolding of time, and especially in relation to the ultimate consequence of the unfolding, which is death.

The Earth, the Circle of Life, underlies and figures into all of these encounters. Yet the Circle goes almost unmentioned in the history of Western philosophy – an omission that is, to my mind, frankly embarrassing. To ask 'Who faces the Circle of Life?' is like a short-form way of asking 'What becomes of the human reality when cast in terms of the encounter with the Circle of Life as an ultimate reality?'

The Human Reality – one should never invoke such august gods unprepared. Let us first acknowledge that there is no such thing as 'human being', writ-large, universal, without condition, without particulars and contexts. Try to imagine a human being without conditions: a human being who has no history, no age, no state of health or illness, no size or shape or weight, no preferences, no interests, no feelings, no thoughts, no date of birth, no name. Not that these conditions are forgotten or hidden or suppressed – rather, imagine a human being who never had them, and still doesn't. You can't do it. It's like trying to think about nothing. You can't do that either. You can think about some volume of empty space, or a pure white or a pure black surface. You can even think about the word 'nothing'. But that is still to think about something. The human being is always being-something. At the very least, the human being is always the being-here, embodied and present at some place and time, and following the narrative of events leading to that place and time. This point would be familiar to those who have read philosophers like Parmenides, David Hume, and The Buddha. Yet it is also a central point in environmental philosophy. The human being dwells in a system of ecological conditions; the human being is always and necessarily an organic, embodied, biological being, embedded in food webs and ecological processes; the human organism is "a transformation-station for energy" (to use Aldo Leopold's words). This dimension of the human being depends upon the surrounding ecology for air, water, food, warmth, and other means of life. Its foundation both lies in the earth and flows from the sun. The ethical, epistemic, and metaphysical significance of humanity's *being-ecological*, as I shall call it from here on, is precisely what environmental philosophy aims to understand.

Yet there are more forms of humanity's being-something than our being-ecological. The human being is also a subjectivity, an unmoved mover for at least some of her actions, a *causa-sui* for at least some of her consciousness: in sum, a *free* being. This is the human being who reasons and knows, who values things and pursues them, who "surges up in the world" (to use Sartre's phrase), who defines herself and defines the meaning of her life. This is the human being conditioned by freedom; the human *being-free*. This condition of the human reality has the most prestige in Western culture and civilization today.

The two forms of being could not be more different. For instance, you could consider the human being-ecological as though it were a mechanism, a function of physics and chemistry, an object. The human being-free cannot be considered so. The relationships among beings-ecological emerge from necessary life-sustaining environmental relations, and not from freedom: for in the absence or depravation of our ecological life-foundations, the possibilities for our being-free diminish, eventually to the point of disappearing entirely, that is, to the point of death. The relationships formed by beings-free, by contrast, are founded upon choices, and upon shared interests, values, and purposes, even if those shared things are also questioned and contested by those who share them.

There is a tension between our being-ecological and our being-free. It is the tension between the being who is a member and plain citizen of the biotic community (to paraphrase Leopold again), and the being who realises herself through reasoning, knowing, valuing, choosing, associating, feeling, identifying, and doing. Those doings, by the way, are *positive freedoms* (following Isaiah Berlin's terms). The free being also realises herself by escaping or removing that which interferes with her exercise of realisation – escaping that which reduces or curtails her range of life-possibilities – *negative freedom*. Positive freedom constitutes civilization itself, as civilization is the process of determining what it means to be human. That determination's ultimate autonomous achievability is always at least partially limited or curtailed by our being-ecological: for we cannot chose not to be air-breathers, or food-eaters. Yet negative freedom also constitutes civilization, too. For civilization has also been the process of repelling or controlling the dangerous faces of nature: protecting ourselves from viruses, animal attacks, severe weather, the darkness of night. On the longest time scale, it is an attempt to liberate ourselves from death, for example by using life-extending technologies such as hygiene, medicine, surgery, and genetic modification.[100] These two freedoms can give the impression that we human beings hold some kind of superiority over animals and over nature.

Further: in Western culture at least since the Enlightenment, we have placed our being-free at the centre of our lives. We place freedom at the foundation of human dignity, moral standing, personal identity, political sovereignty, civil rights, and even Christian salvation. To state it in a single proposition: being-free is the essence of the human spirit. Let us consider the word 'spirit' here not as anything theological, not as a kind of ghost which puppeteers the body or travels to some Otherworld after death. Let us not even consider it as a kind of object. Rather, let us consider it in the older, more primal and more pagan sense of *enacted virtues*, especially heroism and courage, curiosity and wonder, self-expression and revelation. Your spirit is your will to knowledge, to power, to self-creation, to freedom, and to meaning.

The field that draws this spirit closest to our being-free, and at the same time furthest away from our being-ecological, is architecture, the art of building and configuring the physical dimensions of human dwelling. Austrian architect and designer Hans Hollein made this point in a 1968 manifesto called *Absolute Architecture,* where he announced that 'everything is architecture':

Architecture is a spiritual order, realized through building. Architecture – an idea built into infinite space, manifesting man's spiritual energy and power, the material form and expression of his destiny, of his life... All building is religious.[101]

By saying 'religious', Hollein does not mean any particular religious denomination. Rather, he means the will to express ourselves, and to *realize* ourselves in what we express. Architecture does this with stone, metal, mortar, concrete, and glass: materials that can keep their shapes and functions for longer than a human lifetime and so appear to push back against the terror of time and death.[102]

Yet architecture is also removed from our being-ecological because every work of architecture must occupy a plot of territory on the Earth which, after the work is done, becomes a human space and no longer a wilderness. Here's renowned architect Le Corbusier on that point:

Primitive man has brought his chariot to a stop: he decides that here shall be his native soil. He chooses a glade, he cuts down the trees which are too close; he levels the earth around; he opens up the road which will carry him to the river or to those of his tribe whom he has just left... The road is as straight as he can manage with his implements, his arms and his time. The pegs of his tent describe a square, hexagon, or octagon. The palisade forms a rectangle whose four angles are equal. The door of this hut is on the axis of the enclosure... It is the spirit indeed of the Temple of Luxor. There is no such thing as primitive man; there are primitive resources. The idea is constant, in full sway from the beginning.[103]

So architecture, according to Le Corbusier, pushes back, not only against the frontiers of time and death, but also against the frontiers of nature and wilderness. This pushing-back is one way the human spirit works itself out; it's one of the ways we realize ourselves as being-free. Philosopher Karsten Harries, a specialist in the philosophy of art and architecture, summarized both Hollein and Le Corbusier in a single elegant proposition: "to build is to appropriate and humanize nature".[104] Monuments, in particular, according to Harries, "celebrate the time-transcending greatness of the human Spirit as a source of continuing meaning."[105] But any building is a kind of monument in that sense: any building that we raise up, with the intention that it should last, is an act of defiance against the impermanence of things, and thus "an act of spiritual self-assertion".[106]

Apart from a few non-mainstream worldviews that say otherwise, discussions of the human spirit in Western philosophy tend to go as I have described here. They tend *not* to dwell with our being-ecological. When we include our being-ecological in this picture, we find that to build a monument is also to commit future generations to the duty of maintaining, preserving, and repairing it: cutting the grass, pulling up weeds, filling in cracks, expelling animals, and in general holding back the unrelenting creep of time. The moment we grow lax in this duty, or decide not to fulfill it, the green mantle of nature moves in to reclaim its lost sovereignty. Mosses, moulds, insects and fungi move in, followed by animals seeking new dens. Window glass cracks and breaks, wood rots, walls come down. Soils build up, providing more habitat for more plants and animals, burying the building under the earth. Some buildings might remain in the form of crop-marks in farmer's fields, visible only from the air, and often only during a drought. Archaeologists can study them to learn of a building's size and probable function. But a crop-mark is no longer 'an act of spiritual self-assertion'; it is the trace of one, the remainder, the faded shadow. From the point of view of our being-ecological, to build a monument is to begin a struggle with nature which, if we neglect or ignore for too long, nature must win.

Nor is architecture the only source of tension between our being-ecological and our being-free. Our being-ecological, though possessing its own kind of dignity, places us in a trophic structure of symbiote and predator and prey, one species among many, always vulnerable to natural hazards no matter what we do, and subject to evolutionary forces which have no driver and no design. Our being-free attempts to lift us out of that trophic structure. And if not to set us on top of it, our being-free aims to liberate us from it, and place us as far as possible beyond it and apart from it. Our being-free is an expression of the human spirit. Our being-ecological is an expression of the Earth, its ecosystems and organic functions, and the process of natural selection, of evolution. Our being-free says we're special. Our being-ecological says we're not.

At the same time, our being-free opens us to existential matters including the fear of death, and the possibility that life is without meaning. For some people, our being-free, extended to its logical completion, leads to absurdism, if not to nihilism. Meanwhile our being-ecological joins us to systems of life whose ongoing perpetuation of life, and ongoing maintenance of the conditions for life, is a *de facto* proclamation of the desirability of life, a proclamation of life's intrinsic value.

Thus our being-ecological and our being-free are radically different in meaning. Yet both are constitutive of the human being taken as a whole. You see the tension here!

Finally, both of these forms of human being are threatened by the climate crisis, although in different ways. Our being-ecological, having been disrupted by industrial resource extraction and poisoned by consumer and industrial waste-outputs, is now weaponized against us. And our being-free faces a kind of Kantian self-contradiction. For while the climate crisis is, I shall say charitably, no one's deliberate intention, nonetheless it was brought about by an aggregate of free choices made by free beings whose freedom is now diminished precisely because of those freely-made choices. Our being-free is diminished in precise proportion to the damage that the crisis inflicts on our being-ecological, and in proportion to the willed ignorance that our being-free adopts concerning its own responsibility for the crisis.

It is not my aim here to diminish the importance of our being-free, nor to dislodge it from its place in our lives. Rather, my aim is to consider what to do about the tension. I want to understand who we are as human beings, what we have become, what we might become, and what we *should* become, as we face and respond to the Earth, our oasis in the desert of the cosmos, and our home.

Birth: Thrown-ness, Emergence, and Giftedness

We have seen now that human beings have at least two realities: being-ecological, and being-free. But these two realities come in further varieties and conditions. So I think it might be helpful (and also fun) to examine my second root question through a thought experiment: an imagined human life, unfolding over time, encountering all of life's necessary passages, and whatever other milestones may appear on the way. Perhaps this will help illuminate the tension between our two realities, and perhaps that illumination can show us how to heal the broken circle of life.

I shall start with the first moments in which a human being comes to be, and with one possible answer to my second root question which comes from the philosophy of Martin Heidegger. The basic idea is this: we are born from our mothers, into this world – an event and a situation which, for the moment, I shall describe using Heidegger's term: the condition of *thrown-ness*.[107] To explain his idea: Any kind of thinking about the human reality must take place in a situation where the thinker already finds herself alive, present, here on earth, surrounded by various objects and forces, already involved in various relationships with them. We are, in short, thrown into this world, without a plan for it, without any choice about it.

Heidegger says the fact of one's thrown-ness cannot be chosen: we are thrown into the world and, once thrown, are not free to choose not to have been thrown. "As Being, *Dasein* [the human reality] is something that has been thrown [into existence]; it has been brought into its 'there'; but *not* of its own accord."[108] We can only choose how we will go about handling the fact (he uses the word *factity*) of having been thrown.[109] Heidegger's point is, at least, a way of approaching one of the fundamental questions of philosophy: Why are we here? His answer to that question is that we are here for *no* reason; our being-here isn't special, isn't part of anyone's plan.

That's only partly true: Heidegger also says we are thrown into the world already possessing the ability to understand the world; that is, the ability to understand what possibilities arise from our relations with other objects and other beings in the world. We also possess the ability to choose to act upon those possibilities. Those relations and possibilities are also, to be sure, part of what we are thrown into. But chief among them, according to Heidegger, is the relationship with 'fate' and 'destiny', ie. the relationship with the unfolding of time, culminating in death. If, by understanding that fate, we choose to accept it, then we may "take over [our] own thrown-ness" and so seize a kind of freedom.[110] It's a clever philosophical move. It lessens the severity and the arbitrariness of thrownness without denying its basic point; it allows us to imagine that thrownness need not be an unfreedom, even though that is how it was initially defined. We can choose, after the fact, to accept everything we were thrown into. But in that move, Heidegger also says that the most important fact we get thrown into is the fact that we die. And so the most important choice we can make, and the one which entails the most freedom, is to choose to accept death. Thrown-ness, according to Heidegger, can be overcome, and authentic freedom attained, only by embracing death.

But this is rhetorical nonsense. No one embraces freedom by embracing death. Death is the cessation of all forms of being, including the form 'being-free'; it is the extinguishing of the possibility of choosing; the extinguishing of the self who chooses; the extinguishing of all freedoms that the extinguished self might have possessed. It might be argued that Heidegger asks us to accept not death itself, but to accept the *fact* that we die. But that is to affirm part of our being-ecological, and not part of our being-free.

Given Heidegger's membership in the NSDAP, it amuses me to no end that a Jewish philosopher, Emmanuel Lévinas, exposed the nonsense of his position in a public lecture in 1946, in four straightforward sentences:

> I even wonder how the principal trait of our relationship with death could have escaped philosophers' attention. It is not with the nothingness of death, of which we precisely know nothing, that the analysis must begin, but with the situation where something absolutely unknowable appears... death is *ungraspable*, that it marks the end of the subject's virility and heroism. When death is here, I am no longer here, not just because I am nothingness, but because I am unable to grasp.[111]

Someone might counter-argue that there can be a kind of freedom in choosing the time and place of one's own death. Or in refusing to wait for death, or in performing some kind of heroic last deed which, in accomplishing its aims, also kills you. Yet in the same lecture, Lévinas defeats this view with equal ease: "Prior to death there is always a last chance; this is what the hero seizes, not death. The hero is the one who always glimpses a last chance, the one who obstinately finds last chances. Death is thus never assumed; it comes."[112]

Heidegger's presentation of the concept of thrown-ness thus contains an internal contradiction; it refutes itself. What alternatives appear?

- we are *born* into this world.
- we *emerge* into this world.
- we are *given the gift* of existence, of life.
- we are *formed* of the material of this world, by the forces of this world.
- we were *created by the gods,* perhaps *in the image of the gods.*

Suppose we re-frame Heidegger's basic idea in one of these ways. Where might they lead? Any of them might suggest that the appropriate attitude one should assume toward the world is *gratitude.* Think for a moment about exactly what we are 'thrown' *into.* We have all been dropped onto an Earth of staggering wonder and beauty. Of vast oceans, majestic mountains, prismatic autumn forests, wide welcoming savannahs. Of glorious sunshine and glittering starry nights. Of sweet-smelling flowers, and pleasant bird-songs. We are thrown into a human world of parents, siblings, grandparents, aunts and uncles, and cousins – whole crowds of people who love and care from you from the moment they learn of your conception, and without their love you will not even learn to speak nor to walk. Not long after meeting our families we are thrown into a larger human community inhabited by neighbours, shopkeepers, school teachers, nurses, doctors, religious leaders. And friends! After that we are thrown again into still-larger circle of the general public, with its artists, musicians, filmmakers, intellectuals, writers, social reformers, history-makers, and culture-creators; more different kinds of people than you can imagine. We are placed into the flowing throng of history: a rich inheritance of stories, artworks, buildings, religious inspirations, and cultural treasures. And we are thrown into the opportunity to explore all these things. That opportunity does not exist in the counter-factual time before we are thrown; it is also closed to us after death. Thus the release from the unfreedom entailed by thrown-ness is not death: it is the discovery that thrown-ness is not an unfreedom at all. It is, rather, that which opens the very possibility of one's freedom. Indeed it may be a place in human life where our being-free and our being-ecological becomes one.

A counterargument: If you have been given a world of beauty and wonder, so you have also been given a world of danger and terror. For much of the world of nature is also lethal to you: viruses, poisons, parasites, tornadoes, hurricanes, lightning strikes, predatory animals, volcanic eruptions, floods, heat waves. Some of the things we inherit from human culture are also hostile to human life: racism, sexism, prejudices of all kinds, criminality, warfare, murder, slavery, economic exploitation, willed ignorance, and hate, along with the institutions and polities which have supported them. On the widest view, it is clear that the overwhelming majority of the universe is unsurvivable for human life: interstellar space is a radiation-saturated vacuum, for instance. Our sun will explode when it runs out of nuclear fuel. All stars will eventually die out, leaving nothing but black holes. And the whole universe will enter a Great Darkness when the accelerating expansion of spacetime exceeds the speed of light. Given these unhappy facts, is it still tenable to call the world a gift?

There are several ways to answer that objection. One is that the counterargument attempts to weigh the pros and cons of being in the world, and does not look at the matter of being born into the world *as such*. It therefore misses the point of Heidegger's concept as well as my reply to it.

Another answer: perhaps many, if not all, of the things that make the world dangerous can be re-framed as *challenges,* in response to which we flourish; a case could be made that without such challenges we do not flourish to the full extent of our potential. One thinks of the famous Nietzschean proverb: "That which does not kill me makes me stronger." Similarly, Toynbee says civilizations cannot have it too easy, lest they stagnate. But this, too, weighs pros and cons, and does not address the *existential* dimension. It also doesn't address that many people live in circumstances where the 'challenge' is insurmountable by design. Think of people sold into sex-trafficking rings, for example, or locked into poverty by wage-slave jobs and miserly landlords, or forced into refugee camps by a war. They are not 'challenged': they are excluded from their own lives.

A third answer: if we affirm that the world is a gift, then we have to affirm that *all of it* is a gift, including every danger, every horror, every evil thing, every link in the chain of cause-and-effect that helped the world become what it is, no matter how small that help might have been. Again, Nietzsche is our guide here:

> Have you ever said Yes to a single joy? O my friends, then you said Yes to *all* woe. All things are entangled, ensnared, enamored; if ever you wanted one thing twice, if ever you said, "You please me, happiness! Abide, moment!" then you wanted *all* back. All anew, all eternally, all entangled, ensnared, enamored –oh, then you *loved* the world.[113]

Now, that's a very tall order. It may look as if giftedness leads to a self-contradiction similar to the one we saw in Heidegger: the contradiction of treating the suffering and misery of billions of people as if it were a gift. I think the way to understand this reply is to distinguish between contradiction and *tragedy*. A contradiction is an inconsistency in logic: it's the assertion that some proposition and its negation are both true. A tragedy, on the other hand, is a state of affairs in the world. It is a circumstance where all your choices are terrible, but you still have to choose.

Giftedness, as I understand it, has this aura of tragedy. The only way to affirm your being-free without contradiction is to affirm the intrinsic goodness of the world, even while the world so affirmed includes suffering alongside happiness, and darkness alongside light. The alternative, to treat one's own birth as an unfreedom and to treat death as the liberation, leads to only two logically consistent possible ends: mysticism (in the sense that we 'store up our treasures in Heaven' instead of on Earth), or suicide. *Neither of these options will heal the Circle of Life.*

Such is the first part of the answer to the second of my root questions. What human reality emerges from the encounter with the earth? *Tragic giftedness.*

If we were able to grasp a *reason* for the gift, a reason which could also reconcile us to the tragedy, then we might have a grasp on something that deserves to be called an answer to the question "Why are we here?" Such an answer might help us to figure out *the meaning of life.*

Infancy: Seeing, Hearing, Touching, and Knowing

Let's imagine it's a few months after you were born. You can't yet walk or speak, but you're getting to know your world. You're mapping your home in your mind. You're learning to recognise the faces of your family members and some of their friends: the people who will love and care for you during these fragile early years, some of them for the whole of your life.

Sensing the world around you – seeing it, touching it, listening to it, tasting it – is a way of being in relation to it. Yet here it is not enough to say that everyone is in relation with everything they see. The relation to the earth via the marvel of *sentience* requires consistency, familiarity. The possibility of surprise is not ruled out; indeed, never ruled out. Yet a place must be familiar enough that you can make some predictions about it. For instance, you can make some broad decisions about what to do in and with that place, decisions that benefit from knowledge of what has happened there in the past and what is most likely to happen again in the future. And that knowledge requires time. In that sense getting to know a place is like getting to know a person. As you observe and interact with someone new over weeks and months, you get a general image of how they move and speak, what their habits and wants and aversions are, how they might respond to your choices, whether it's safe or dangerous to be near them, and so on. So it is with places. One cannot know a forest by walking it only once. It takes several full cycles of the seasons, and regular explorations during that time, preferably daily, to even *begin* to know a place. Where are its berry trees and when are the berries ripe? Where are its meltwater ponds in the spring? Where is the nearest raccoon den, and how often do you normally see them out and about? When do the maple trees change colour for autumn? When will there be a mast year for acorns? Such are the habits of landscapes. It takes many years to get to know them. Some people may get a head-start in this process, benefitting from the guidance of grandparents, local elders, and other community leaders; though as observed earlier, the climate crisis can disrupt the old familiar cycles of nature, rendering this kind of ancestral knowledge less helpful.

This kind of relationship with the earth rests upon what I call *perceptual intelligence:* a highly complex and subtle form of reasoning in which:

1. Almost every cell in the body gathers, records, and transmits information about the state of the surrounding environment. The information covers a wide variety of factors including temperature, the shapes and colours of clouds and water waves and sunlight, the sounds of birds and rustling leaves and creaking tree trunks; the sense of air pressure building up or ebbing away, the smells and tastes in the air, the sense of cardinal direction, and (very possibly) magnetic fields and electric charges.[114]

2. Deep in the subconscious mind, the current state of all that information is compared to memories of other occasions when the state of the environment was similar.

3. That comparison allows you to make broad predictions about what is happening just out of sight and/or how things might change over the next few hours.

4. Predictions are communicated to the conscious mind in the form of feelings, hunches, aversions, and attractions.[115]

Rupert Ross, an attorney who served various First Nations communities across Canada, learned from his Indigenous friends and associates that this kind of intelligence was an essential part of their way of life, both historically and today. As he described it:

The hunter-gatherer did his shopping in the natural world. As already noted, his success depended upon his ability to accurately read the innumerable variables which each season, day and hour presented. Those variables, however, presented patterns which, over time and with great attention, one could learn to recognize. Reading those patterns to determine when "the time was right" was the essential life skill, and it constituted, in my view, a very specialized form of thought.[116]

Anyone who takes the time and who has the patience can do it. Ross himself learned to do it, while working as a fishing guide in Northern Ontario. Early in the morning of each day, he would stand by the dock for half an hour to get a "feel" for the day, which would tell him which part of the lake to take his clients, so they had a better chance to make good catches:

I made mental notes about such things as wind speed and direction, cloud cover, temperature... the quality of the light, the humidity, the sense of disturbance-building or disturbance-waning... In truth I simply cannot list all of the things that were finally incorporated into this "feel" for the day. I don't believe that they ever came to my conscious attention, but they were noticed all the same... What I look for, of course, is correspondence between what I anticipate and what I recall.[117]

It's worth noting that although this activity might look and feel like mysticism, there is nothing supernatural about it. As Ross said, it is "without doubt, a very complex and compacted form of reasoning."[118] Ross and his community learned this in a boreal forest, but perceptual intelligence can work in any kind of environment. Even in the ocean, there is information enough for the body to gather and process, to tell a navigator how far they are from land, which direction to the nearest or largest chain of islands, which direction the deepest ocean currents are moving, whether a storm is coming and how heavy it will be. Canadian anthropologist Wade Davis recorded how perceptual intelligence allowed the Polynesian people to explore and colonize the entire Pacific Ocean, maintaining political alliances and trade routes, and navigating with accuracy, beyond the sight of land, without using a compass or a sextant or a satellite GPS network:

> The truly great navigators... can identify the presence of distant atolls of islands beyond the visible horizon simply by watching the reverberation of waves across the hull of the canoe, knowing full well that every island group in the Pacific has its own refractive pattern that can be read with the same ease with which a forensic scientist would read a fingerprint.[119]

It might be controversial for me to say it, but I think the logic points me this way: perceptual intelligence is the root of humanity's being-ecological, *more so* than the fact that we must eat, drink, and breathe from the biosphere. We human beings are "already ecological" because our perceptual intelligence grants us the ability to gather deep knowledge of our surroundings. This is likely the root of many forms of symbiosis between animals, too. This knowledge is 'deep' in the sense that it requires years of patience and consistent attendance to gather, and requires the sentience of your whole body to process and to reason toward conclusions. This, I think, is a deeper form of being-ecological than eating and breathing because it configures and informs our lives, not only in the physical dimension of continued bodily survival, but also in the intimate and subtle dimension of consciousness. We *think and feel* the ways that we do because of the work of perceptual intelligence, constantly feeding our bodies and minds with information about the habits and the ways of the places where we spend the most time. To put it loosely, but in a way that surely gets the point across: the more you get to know a landscape, the more the landscape rubs off on your mind, massaging it, working it over, planting seeds in it, pushing its footprints into it. Eventually the landscape becomes so much a feature of your mind that it also becomes a feature of your *identity*. It gets that far when a complete account of *who you are* must necessarily include a few statements about the places where you possess this kind of deep knowledge, the time you spent acquiring it, and the things you've done in your life because of it.

Of course, it follows from this argument that you can have this kind of deep knowledge of human worlds, too. The ways and habits of families, colleagues from work, neighbours, friends, congregants at your place of worship if you are religious, and so on, can also massage your mind no less than landscapes and climates can do.

And, furthermore, it also follows that you *cannot* have deep knowledge of a landscape if your encounter with it is only occasional and superficial. I have to say it again: it takes time –

years, many years – to gather the kind of deep knowledge I speak of here. But if it's any consolation: those years can be remarkably pleasurable. Bird song, for example, reduces stress and lifts emotions. Researchers in Germany found that "the individual enjoyment of life is correlated to the number of bird species in one's surroundings. An additional ten percent of bird species in the vicinity therefore increases the life satisfaction of Europeans at least as much as a comparable increase in income."[120] Researchers from UCSF found that older adults who took fifteen-minute walks in a forest for eight consecutive weeks reported less stress, more calm, and more awe, in their lives. The researchers asked participants to post 'selfie' photos during their walks, and they found that over time the selfies had more emphasis on landscapes and surroundings, and brighter smiles.[121] It is probably not the case that nature has an intrinsic power to calm us. Rather, as the researchers in the study of older adults noted, it's more likely that the positive emotional affects come about from "shifting our energy and attention outward instead of inward."[122]

Let me sum up this meditation with a second answer to the root question. What human reality emerges from the encounter with the earth? *A state of being-ecological, informed by perceptual intelligence and deep knowledge, which in turn informs selfhood and identity.*

Childhood: The Naming of the World

Let's imagine it's around a year after your birth. You're learning to walk. And you're learning how to make words. You're building relationships in your mind between a complex array of the sounds people make, which way their eyes and hands point when they make those sounds, what shapes their faces make, whether the sounds come loud and fast or soft and gentle, and how people respond when you make sounds of your own. Pointing-and-vocalizing behaviour, widely regarded among contemporary linguists as the source of language both for children and for our most ancient hominid ancestors, was once thought to be distinctly human. But it has been observed in other primates in the wild, especially chimpanzees.[123] All of these associations will create emotional and cognitive phenomena in your mind which will go on to inform everything you think and feel and do for the rest of your life: the phenomena of crafting and sharing meaning through audio-visual symbolism: the phenomena of language.

In the book of Genesis, God charges Adam to give names to all the animals. This, said Karsten Harries, is a way of humanizing the natural world: "To feel at home in paradise Adam first had to make what God created his own. Adam's first naming was an act of appropriation."[124] So language, we can say, is a function of humanity's being-free. In fact it is arguably more central to humanity's being-free than architecture and construction. Imagine, for example, attempting to design a civilization without the ability to talk to other people. You might be able to do basic hunting and gathering, and you might be able to play music on simple instruments. But you could not have poetry, or a farmer's market, or farms, or anything requiring a sequence of tasks to be completed in a certain order. It is possible to have civilization without cities; it is not possible to have civilization without language.

Could language also arise from our being-ecological? The most influential present-day affirmation of this idea comes from David Abram, author of *The Spell of the Sensuous* (1996), who argued that spoken words arose from "our original sensory participation with the enveloping natural field." Here's a summary of his hypothesis, in his own words:

If we listen, first, to the sounds of an oral language – to the rhythms, tones, and inflections that play through the speech of an oral culture – we will likely find that these elements are attuned in multiple and subtle ways to the contour and scale of the landscape, to the depth of its vales or the open stretch of its distances, to the visual rhythms of the local topography.

But the human speaking is necessarily tuned, as well, to the various nonhuman calls and cries that animate the local terrain. Such attunement is simply imperative for any culture still dependent upon foraging for its subsistence.[125]

Darwinian selection might have something to do with this. In 1926 the ecologist Hans Stadler found that the songs of forest birds contain more whistles and pure tones, whereas open grassland birds sing with more trills.[126] He theorized that the acoustic properties of a given environment – competing sounds from other organisms, noise from the wind in the trees, acoustic absorption or reflection properties of soil or rock or plant life – naturally selects for sounds that can carry across the needed distances in that environment. But Abram's view is not Darwinian as such. He says that "a subtle sort of onomatopoeia is constantly at work in language: certain meanings inevitably gravitate toward certain sounds, and vice versa."[127] He gives the example of the Koyukon phrase meaning 'It is a fine evening', which imitates the cheerful and grateful song of the hermit thrush.[128] This dimension of language, Abram says, has never been forgotten by poets and artists, nor by those whose lives remain close to the Earth.

So, those are two ways that language figures into my root question: in the first, language claims and humanizes the natural world; in the other, language emerges from the natural world and binds us to it. It might be tempting to say that Abram's view is better, because it could help us reclaim a deep relationship that humans once had with the Earth, and which we might need to reclaim in order to heal the broken Circle of Life. But the political usefulness of an idea cannot be the whole of its rational justification. As the founder of Deep Ecology, Arne Naess, wrote: "it is indecent for a teacher to proclaim an ethic for tactical reasons only".[129]

I am going to pursue a third way of relating language to my root question. The words you use, the way you learn them, and the way you use them, are indicators of something. With that in mind, consider the following words: *acorn, adder, bluebell, bramble, conker, dandelion, fern, heather, heron, ivy, kingfisher, lark, magpie, newt, otter, raven, starling, weasel, willow,* and *wren.* Are there any words on this list that you don't know? (Don't be embarrassed about it. In several of the classes I teach at my college, I recite this list to my students, all of them adults, and no one knows them all.) For each of the words on this list that you don't know, consider a few questions: What could you guess about it based on other words from the list that you do know? What do you think it names? Where might you find it? Is it beautiful? Dangerous? Friendly? Skittish? Clever? Strong? Rare? Common? Might you have encountered one already without knowing its name? Also, notice what is happening in your mind as you consider those questions. A cluster of phenomena forms. Expectations build. And with them, various feelings: perhaps curiosity, or fear, or impatience, or wistfulness. Psychologists have found that word-sounds often carry emotional resonances which influence what we think and feel about the objects and events that the word-sounds name. Words with more hard consonants suggest something rough, heavy, and sharp; words with more soft consonants suggest something smooth, round, and gentle.[130] It's similar to how people tend to associate emotions with colours; globally, people tend to associate the same colours with the same feelings.[131] This much likely emerges from our being-ecological: they are the phonemes that seem suggested or prompted by our surroundings.

But at the same time, the words we assign to things also configure how we think about those things and how we relate to them. Consider the following two sentences:

1. "He lived in a charming rustic cottage."
2. "He lived in a rickety old shack."

And let us say, *ex hypothesi*, that both statements describe the exact same house. Yet words like 'rustic' and 'charming' convey a different impression than words like 'old' and 'rickety'. Those different impressions, in turn, convey a different sense of reality, a different sense of the truth. To show this with another example: researchers found that the words 'north' and 'south' convey different impressions about ease of movement: people tend to think it will take longer to travel north than south, or that it will cost more to ship something to a northern destination than to a southern. It's an artifact of the way we tend to orient maps with north at the top: going south feels more like going downhill.[132] To choose another example: psychologists found that participants playing a Prisoner's Dilemma type game played more competitively when they were told it was called 'The Wall Street Game', and played more cooperatively when told the exact same game was called 'The Community Game'.[133] Words and names configure attitudes and realities; different configurations of words and names lead people to make different decisions about what to believe, and what to do. And this dimension of language emerges from our being-free.

As I hope you found in this exercise, words do not stand alone as symbols or references for objects. They also come embedded in webs of relations: to the beings, objects, and events that they name, to the other things involved in their functioning or their properties, the feelings and needs associated with them, to memories and stories involving them, to the contexts or situations in which they are typically encountered, and so on. I shall here call this web of relationships *a field of life*.

A word is a name for a field of life. The fields of life are sometimes easier to see when we find out it has a name. So, to change examples, think about music performed in a language you don't understand. You may not know the exact reference to the words. You might get a glimpse of the *sense* of the words: the emotional tones, the activities and events, the colours. That glimpse is not the full spectacle. But it is enough for the unknown words to act as the threshold for many fields of life that are open for you to explore by learning the words. And it is enough for the unknown words to signify *that there is a field of life*, as yet unknown to you, which you might someday explore.

Why, then, do we learn some words and not others? A simple answer might be: we learn the words that belong to the fields of life in which we happen to dwell. Some we learn from adults when we were children; some we learn on our own. Does it follow that when we do not know a word, it is because we do not dwell in the field of life that the word comes from? Not necessarily. You could learn words that belong to fields of life in which you do not dwell. But by learning such a word, that field of life becomes part of your world, even if only in some small, temporary way. And the more often you use the word, the more you draw that field of life into your world, and the more you come to dwell in that field of life.

We can also dwell in fields of life for which we do not have the words. For example, I can live in a city where I don't know the names of all its streets, nor the names of its most common architectural styles. But the longer we dwell in a given field of life, the more likely it is that we will find words for the beings and events who dwell there. Suppose I move to a country cottage, where many different kinds of birds dwell in the surrounding fields and forests. If I do not know their names, I'll eventually create my own: I'll call them the big loud black ones, the flitty little yellow ones, the ones that look like the black ones but they're smaller and their heads are bluer.[134] By naming them so, I invite them into my world; I designate them as something relevant to me, no matter the kind of relevance, utilitarian or aesthetic, and even if that relevance is small. In sum: we learn words because of the relevance of the fields of life that they name.

Yet we cannot name the world without the cooperation of others. If I asked you to meet me at the Three Brothers, and 'The Three Brothers' is a name that I made up myself, you might gather that I am referring to a place, because of the *sense* of the word; its relation to other words in the sentence. But you wouldn't know where it is, nor even *what* it is. Is it a mountain peak? A hillock in a forest? A restaurant? A statue in a city park? Is it in the real world or in a computer-generated simulation of a world? As long as it's a private name, you cannot answer those questions; and as long as you cannot answer those questions, you cannot meet me there, and so you cannot share in that part of my world. Words thus open other people as fields of life in their own respect.

A digression. A popular yet incorrect interpretation of the Buddhist principle of Name-And-Form says that words isolate things and break their relations with the rest of the world. This is not so. It may appear that by learning the name of some field of life, we limit, reduce, or isolate that field of life to that name. But it is not the case that every word corresponds to only one field of life. Similarly, many fields of life have more than one name. Indeed, the more names a field of life possesses, the richer that field becomes in meaning as the different names show how various fields of life overlap with each other. And so, the richer our lives become for being able to share those meanings. Imagine a language in which every word referred to every field of life, all at once, simultaneously. In that language, you would have to use the exact same words to praise, blame, offend, love, request help, make promises, break promises, lie, teach, thank, quote, command, or do anything else that we do with words. Everyone would live in a constant state of confusion concerning what was said, what was heard, what was intended. And no one could express their confusion or misunderstanding to each other. All knowledge would consist of pure qualia, passed over in silence until we all died from eating poisoned mushrooms that we couldn't warn each other about. Besides that: if the correct word for a given field of life is something like 'suffering', or 'injustice', or 'climate emergency', then we have to be able to say so if we are to do anything about it. And we should not have to hedge the statement with disclaimers and apologies.

Now, look again at the list of twenty words that I gave earlier. What I didn't mention, and what I need to mention now, is that they are twenty of the nature-based words cut from the Oxford Junior Dictionary in 2017, to widespread outrage among writers and environmentalists.[135] Fields of life do not disappear when their names disappear. But when a field of life no longer appears relevant to us, the names fall out of use. *Language acts here as the measure of a community's engagement with a field of life.* Hence, words associated with urban and modern fields of life were added to the dictionary: words like *blog, broadband, bullet point, chatroom, MP3 player,* and *voice mail.*[136] Incidentally, words associated with religion and the monarchy, such as *aisle, bishop, empire,* and *sin,* were also cut out: another indicator of the changing interests and attentions of contemporary British culture.[137]

To be sure, language is not an *exact* measure of a community's engagement with life. We still use words and phrases from fields of life that we no longer live in. For instance, we still say someone is 'fighting in the trenches' or 'going over the top' even though the First World War ended more than a hundred years ago. But the measure is precise *enough* to reveal noteworthy trends in culture, society, politics, economics, and consciousness. The curators of the Oxford Junior Dictionary made the decision to cut those words because British children do not spend much time in nature anymore. A study by Britain's National Trust found that fewer than 10% of British children play in wild spaces as a regular part of their lives: this is down from 40% of the previous generation.[138] Japanese researchers found that children have more fear of nature than previous generations, including negative attitudes toward harmless creatures like butterflies. The same researchers also found a correlation between decreasing time spend in nature and increasing fear of it.[139] Much as I found the cutting of nature words from the OJD lamentable, I also found it informative. Dictionaries, like libraries and theatres and related craft-houses of language, are measuring-rods of cultural change.

Language can serve that way *even when language obscures,* rather than reveals, the realities of a field of life. Events impress themselves upon us, virtually demanding to be named: and yet some events are uncomfortable, disruptive, too big to comprehend in simple terms, or in some other way threatening to our worldviews or our projects. And so we grant those unwelcome events names which will soothe our ruffled feathers and reassure our thumping hearts that there's nothing to worry about, and that all shall soon be well. Consider the following pairs of phrases, one of which is the reality, the other is the euphemism which conceals the reality and reassures both listener and speaker that the reality is not painful and that everything is under control.[140]

Euphemism:	*Reality:*
He lives in a low-income neighbourhood	He lives in a slum
The company is downsizing	The company is firing people
She has post-traumatic stress disorder	She is traumatised
He passed away	He is dead

Euphemisms reveal the state of the language-community's social, political, and cultural priorities, possibly also its psychological condition, through what fields of life they select for concealment and reassurance. This is so because euphemism-words and reality-words which refer to the exact same set of material facts can at the same time conjure very different social, political, emotional, and imaginal fields of life.

Here are some examples from the field of environmental policy. One column describes the reality of the destruction of the earth; the other, the euphemisms which conceal humanity's agency in that destruction, and which reassure us that business-as-usual may continue without interruption and without significant consequences.[141]

Euphemism:	*Reality:*
Climate change	Climate crisis, climate emergency
Global warming	Global heat wave
Wilderness, undeveloped land	The Earth
Fish stocks	Fish populations
Fossil fuel	Greenhouse gas source
Biodiversity	Life, wildlife
Ecosystem services	Life-support systems
Natural capital	Nature
Natural infrastructure	Mountain, forest, wetland, grassland, etc.
Natural resources	Gifts of the Earth
Sustainable development	Uninterrupted exploitation of nature
Species extinction, biodiversity loss	Genocide, ecocide, murder
Landscape or resource development	Landscape destruction
Deforestation	Forest destruction
Emissions and externalities	Poisons
The New Normal	A state of permanent crisis
The Environment	Our home
Disproportionate impacts	The poor die first
Private research foundation, think-tank	Lobby group with undisclosed financial backers
Think globally act locally	Do not disrupt global capitalism
Reduce, reuse, recycle	Do not lobby for comprehensive social change

You might think that some of my word-choices for reality are 'extreme' or 'too much', or that they 'go too far'. That reaction is also, in its own way, a euphemism. More precisely, it's a strategy of uncritical dismissal, whose purpose is to prevent people from thinking too deeply about realities revealed by dispelled euphemisms. When a newly revealed reality prompts new ethics dilemmas and new demands for justice, the dismissive euphemism of 'that's an extreme opinion' helps ensure that those dilemmas remain unconsidered, and the demands for justice remain unheeded. It follows from the logic of that most insidious and deep-seated of illusions which civilization often instills in people's minds: *the illusion of No Alternative*.[142] Under that illusion, the necessary remedies remain unthinkable, and the crisis carries on.

So far, I have shown how words and languages act as measuring-rods for the state of a community. Yet the examples of the euphemisms show that the state of a community can also influence the appearance of the world. Names configure how we think about things, how we relate to them, how we feel about them, the significance we assign to them, and thus what we do about them. Different names for *the exact same phenomena* produce different feelings, and call for different responses. Words, realities, and actions thus influence each other in a mutual circle of configuration, a feedback loop, an ecosystem with three members. To my mind, this suggests that language is a force in humanity's being-ecological whose working-out over time contributes to changes in the state of human culture *and* the state of the earth, in a manner comparable to the phenomena that ecologists call *ecosystem succession*. The ecosystem of language, action, and reality works itself out much the same as the ecosystems of the Earth: over time, it changes its state, thus producing new human cultures living upon new ecological foundations.

Now, look again at the reality-words and euphemism-words

relating to environmental policy. If a community were to speak of climate events using only the euphemism-words, or only the reality-words, what future human culture could follow? We can graph the possibilities on a decision matrix, in the style of Pascal's Wager, as follows:

	The climate crisis is not real	The climate crisis is real
We speak of it using reality-words	We re-tool the economy to favour renewable energy, less waste, etc., resulting in cleaner air and water, but otherwise politics and business carries on as usual.	We re-tool the economy to favour renewable energy, less waste, etc., resulting in cleaner air and water, healthier children, preserved forests, fewer tropical storms, etc.
We speak of it using uphemism-words	Politics and business carries one as usual.	Air and water continues to toxify, waste continues growing, children's health deteriorates, forests disappear, tropical storms intensify, more pandemic diseases emerge, more people die from heat waves, etc.

If the climate crisis is real, that ecosystem of language, action, and reality will work toward one of two possible climax states, depending on how language acts within it: one in which we live in a profoundly different *but still living* ecosystem of earth and culture; the other in which we die.

What, then, to do? As a start: we should reject the euphemisms, and adopt the language of reality. That way, we may more easily see the real consequences of our actions, and also more easily see what else needs to be done.

Such is a third answer to the first of my root questions. What human reality emerges from the encounter with the earth? *An ecological succession of cultures, measured by, and at the same time driven by, language.*

Childhood: Innocence And Play

My first forest was a sugar maple forest near Ayton, Ontario, that my grandparents bought for their retirement home. My family visited many times a year for a week at a time, and often for longer. In the summer, the visits coincided with some of the extended family visiting at the same time, so my siblings and I could play with our cousins. We built forts in the trees, and tore down the forts built by the local boy scouts. We fished in the Rocky Saugeen river, and raced each other along the trails Grandad cut through the bush to make way for his tractor. While there was family everywhere during these visits, still I often explored the forest on my own. I had my favourite hiding places, where I could daydream without interruption. (I spent a lot of that time imagining that I had come to this planet from outer space, but that is another story.) About a week before my ninth birthday, my family moved to the village of Elora. There I found a new forest to explore: the Elora Gorge Conservation Park. Along with my grandparent's forest, the Gorge became part of my imaginal wonderland: it was my Tir na nOg, my Shire, my Narnia, my Fellwater.

Nor am I the only adult to notice that childhood play in the forest often produces adult love of the forest. Here's George Eliot, the pen-name of Mary Anne Evans, in *The Mill On The Floss* (1860):

We could never have loved the earth so well if we had had no childhood in it, if it were not the earth where the same flowers come up again every spring that we used to gather with our tiny fingers as we sat lisping to ourselves on the grass, the same hips and haws on the autumn hedgerows, the same redbreasts that we used to call 'God's birds' because they did no harm to the precious crops. What novelty is worth that sweet monotony where everything is known and loved because it is known?

And here's the Puerto Rican poet William Carlos Williams, whose first "thronging memories" are of a forest in New Jersey, at a time when the state was more rural than urban:

Kipp's woods, just over the back fence, was our wilderness... I knew every tree in that wood, from the hickory where a squirrel had its hole to the last dogwood where in the fall the robins would gather for the red berries they are so fond of... What I learned was the way the moss climbed about a tree's roots, what growing dogwood and iron wood looked like; the way rotten leaves will mat down in a hole – and their smell when turned over – every patch among those trees had its character, moist or dry... Kipp's woods was my magic forest.[143]

Nor are poets and writers the only ones to notice this. Psychologists, too, have found that childhood time in nature contributes to adult spiritual development: self-awareness, kindness, and reverence.[144] This is not an universal experience, of course. Plenty of people have childhoods in or near forests and yet they grow into adults who no longer care about the Earth. But I think this experience is sufficiently common that I can stake the following conjecture: There's something special about a childhood full of nature.

But what exactly is that specialness? What is it about a forest that makes it for a child a magic forest?

There are deep roots in the Western canon for the idea that

childhood is a special time of life. For instance, in the gospel of Luke, Jesus said: "I praise you, Father, Lord of heaven and earth, because you have hidden these things from the wise and learned, and revealed them to little children." (Luke 10:21). Similarly, Jesus told his followers, "Let the little children come to me, and do not hinder them, for the kingdom of heaven belongs to such as these." (Matt 19:14). To be sure, other passages in the New Testament call upon us to grow up. But what special wisdom does God reveal to children? Why does the kingdom of heaven belong to them? And must it belong to *only* children – can it not also belong to adults?

We have to wait until Montaigne and Rousseau before we get a serious philosophical attempt to answer such questions. Rousseau, the better known of the two, thought that childhood was a time of *innocence*. He wrote that parents and educators should:

> Love childhood, promote its games, its pleasures, its amiable instinct. Who among you has not sometimes regretted that age when a laugh is always on the lips and the soul is always at peace? Why do you want to deprive these *little innocents* of the enjoyment of a time so short which escapes them and of a good so precious which they do not know how to abuse? Why do you want to fill with bitterness and pains these first years which go by so rapidly and can return no more for them than they can for you? Fathers, do you know the moment when death awaits your children? Do not prepare regrets for yourself in depriving them of the few instants nature gives them. As soon as they can sense the pleasure of being, arrange it so that they can enjoy it, arrange it so that at whatever hour God summons them they do not die without having tasted life.[145]

Innocence – children as 'little innocents' – a word as heavily burdened with moral and epistemic baggage as the word 'nature' itself, which Rousseau would also redefine in his time. Yet from this passage and others like it, we grasp that by 'innocence' Rousseau means something like a state of happiness and peace that is short-lived, fragile, and, importantly, *our natural state;* that is, a state which adult concerns, especially the fear of death, can damage.

Other passages in the text suggest that Rousseau regarded childhood as a state of pre-rational consciousness; to put it another way, children do not reason like adults do, and shouldn't be expected to. As he puts it:

Nature wants children to be children before being men. If we want to pervert this order, we shall produce precocious fruits which will be immature and insipid and will not be long in rotting. We shall have young doctors and old children. Childhood has its ways of seeing, thinking, and feeling which are proper to it. Nothing is less sensible than to want to substitute ours for theirs, and I would like as little to insist that a ten-year-old be five feet tall as that he possess judgment.[146]

What does all this discussion of childhood and innocence have to do with the search for our human reality in relation to the earth? Three things, as follows:

First, it's a possible answer to the question that opened this chapter. Perhaps 'innocence' is the quality that allows children to turn forests into kingdoms of magic.

Second, Rousseau believed that the countryside was the best environment for preserving children's natural innocence for as long as possible. He concluded that Emile should be raised "in the country... far from the black morals of cities which are covered with a veneer seductive and contagious for children".[147]

And third, if Rousseau was correct about childhood, it might follow that any statement a child makes about the Earth, or about their relation to it, could be treated as a statement about the natural condition of humanity's relation to the Earth. There have been many philosophical studies of children's ideas about nature, as well as studies of how their ideas interact with their communities. Some of these studies involved interviewing children, or showing them photographs and artifacts and then recording their free associations. Some involved giving children cameras and letting them loose in a forest, then studying the photos they took.[148] One pilot study found that when children are allowed to freely associate, they define nature in ways most adults do not. Here are some of the things the children in that study had to say:

- "Nature is everything that the humans have not made."
- "Nature is used for the production of artifacts."
- "Nature is development, growing and vanishing."
- "Nature is renewing itself, even after natural disaster."
- "Nature is the cycle of life."
- "Nature is evil."
- "The human is part of nature."
- "Nature is the entire universe."
- "Nature is the organization of all living things living together."
- "Nature as the provider of good."
- "Nature as the provoker of aesthetic judgements."
- "Nature as a higher order creative and spiritual force."
- "The inherent part of the nature of humans is to create culture."
- "Humans are part of nature because they descended from the apes."[149]

If the same experiment was done with different children and in different places, different results might follow. The researchers themselves acknowledged that a child's proximity to green-grass playgrounds, and to forests, could influence the results. Nonetheless, taking what we have here, I'm intrigued by the way some of the children attributed *intentionality* to natural functions: the children said nature is a 'creative force', 'renewing itself', 'developing, growing, and vanishing', 'good', and 'evil'. This is an attitude toward nature that we do not find in most adults. Recalling my hypothesis: perhaps the personifying attitude, involving concepts like 'balance of nature', 'Mother Nature', and a 'circle of life', is part of the innocence of childhood; a way of facing the earth which, even if not all children possess it, most adults somehow lose.

There's another feature of childhood, besides innocence, that we should consider here, and which as adults we also tend to lose: *play*. Sure, some adults do 'play' in a broad sense: they go on holidays, they throw parties, they do things for fun that they don't do for work. In the forest, we go camping, hiking, skiing, rock climbing, spelunking, swimming, snowshoeing, running, cycling, lovemaking, and so on. All of these activities are, obviously, different kinds of play. But consider the reasons we give for why we do these things as adults. We go to the forest to 'recharge', or to 'wind down' after a hard day at the office – notice the vocabulary of machine-function here. We go to the forest to get exercise, to de-stress ourselves, and to promote health and longevity. We go to the forest to appraise the value of its sights and sounds; to approve or disapprove of its authentic naturalness; the eco-tourist is a kind of quality-control inspector. And we go to the forest to 'escape', to 'get a breath of fresh air', to 'get away from it all'. What each of these reasons have in common is their essentially instrumental character. We do these things as adults because of some benefit we hope it will bring to some other field of our lives.[150]

How unusual and how rare it is when an adult says she goes into the forest because she loves the forest. How remarkable, even *uncomfortable*, when an adult says she goes to the forest because she is a forest creature. Adults are expected to be creatures of civilization and not of nature. That means, among other things, adults are expected to regard the earth as a field of resources to take, dangers to neutralize, services to receive, and space to claim – that's if we bother to think of nature at all. Adult men, especially, are expected to *want* things and to *own* things, more than to love things. This instrumental rationale for play is almost always beautifully missing from the lives of children.

The overwhelming majority of professional research about child play emphasizes its benefits for adult life,[151] such as its contribution to brain development, skill acquisition, resilience, teamwork, competition, fairness, graciousness in winning and losing, and parental bonding.[152] All very well and good – but none of these understand the truth about child play. What is distinctive about child play is its *intrinsic meaning:* for children, play is an end-in-itself. Some studies do acknowledge that play "does not seem to serve any apparent immediate purpose,"[153] yet the lack of instrumental meaning tends to appear in the research as something of an aporia. Some researchers say that the nature of play requires a "multidimensional approach" to its definition.[154] But that only means the definition will be a long compound sentence. I'm snarking about this because it's important. The majority of adults do not treat recreation as an intrinsic good, which is almost the same as saying *they've forgotten how to play*.

It is play, I think, and not innocence, which transforms a forest into a kingdom of magic. For it is play – pleasurable activities having the structure of a narrative and carried on primarily for their own sake – which allows a tallgrass meadow, a flight of birds, a butterfly sighting, a long summer sunset, to assume a greater range of meaning than is possible without it. I'm making a statement about the nature of *magic* here, as much as I'm making a statement about landscapes and ecologies: *magic is a function of meaning*.[155] The wider the possible ranges of meaning that something may assume, then the more magical it can be. The narrower the ranges of its possible meanings, as when an object's meaning is to serve some utilitarian purpose, then the less magical it can be. Think of an ordinary object that you might find in almost anyone's home: something like a hammer. If your purpose is utilitarian, such as to drive a nail into a wall, then the hammer can be only one thing: a hammer. It might have the additional meaning of being your father's old hammer that he gave to you, or it's the hammer that you used when you helped your best friend fix up his house. Nonetheless, when your intentions with the hammer are primarily instrumental, the hammer's meaning remains primarily instrumental. But suppose you are playing a fantasy game with a child. Now the hammer might be Mjolnir, the Hammer of Thor. A moment later, it's a control stick in the cockpit of a space ship. A moment after that, it's a conductor's baton, and you're conducting a song playing on the radio: further, the radio becomes the band, performing under your direction. I've used the example of child role-playing and pretending, but I think the point holds for any activity that can be enriched by approaching it as a form of play: performing theatre, playing most types of sports and games, telling jokes, creating and sharing music and art, religious seeking, daydreaming. Even higher education and scientific research, when guided by the ever-elusive 'love of learning', is a kind of play. The space that surrounds you, and the objects within it, can take on any *meaning* that supports the play. If their material properties don't change, nonetheless their meanings can change as fluidly and as surprisingly as any magic wand.

Since this is a meditation on landscapes and climates and ecologies, I am led to wonder: is there something special about the kind of play, and the kind of magic, that can be had in a forest? Do natural settings lend themselves to magic more easily or more readily than houses, urban neighbourhoods, schools, daycares, or other features of civilization?

In at least one way, they do. A natural setting is, by definition, a space not crafted by human hands. It's a space whose contours came about on their own. It's home to animals who make their own intentionalities, their own purposes, their own *encounter with you*, as much as you can make your encounter with them. Its trees, shrubs, grasses, fungi, and mosses are *living things in their own right*: they are born, reveal themselves, grow, change, and disappear again, all according to their own ways of being in the world. And what are those ways? What laws, what powers, do they follow? Where did they come from, and what might they do next? Such dramatic questions inform the many meanings that a tree, a landmark or landscape, a wild animal, and the like, could assume under the aspect of play. To put it another way: when approached under the aspect of play, a natural setting becomes a field of dramatic discovery. A human setting, such as a house or an urban neighbourhood, can be a field of discovery too, but the answers to its dramatic questions inevitably refer back to something human. In the forest, the answers can refer back to something *other-than-human*. This, I think, makes its potential for magic greater.

Not that this necessarily makes the dramatic discoveries in natural settings better, or worse, than those that can be found in the human world; for the moment, it's enough to say it makes them different. (A childhood without natural magic might be incomplete: whole ranges of discovery and wonder would be missing from such a life, and there would be the tragedy of not knowing what was missing.)

Not only different; the magic of the forest won't always be *safe*. Some dramatic discoveries in the forest will be animals or swarms of insects that can hurt you if provoked. Some will be cliff sides and sink holes where you might fall, or rushing rivers that could carry you away to drown. Some might be the sudden advent of rough weather: winds blowing tree branches into your face, hard rain sapping your body heat, an earthquake breaking the ground on which you stand. The human realm can be dangerous, too: the collapse of a wall in a ruined house that you're exploring, the threats of a possessive property-owner when you're crossing his back yard, are also dramatic discoveries of a sort. But as mentioned, those discoveries refer back to the human world. In the forest, the dramatic discoveries can refer back to the more-than-human: they can refer to something *inexplicable in human terms*. Even if you and your child are pretending that a room in your house is a forest, still that imaginal forest must have the dimensions of the room; an imaginal forest explored in an actual forest can have the dimensions of a forest.

Over the last twelve years I have walked every trail, every hill-crest, every stream-edge within a two-hour walking radius of my house: everything between Lac-Des-Fees and Pink Lake, and a little beyond. Even so, in all that time, I still encounter things I never knew about before. Last year I saw a Great Horned Owl in the park for the first time. Its swift yet stately flight above my head caught my eye; a dark shadow in front of the sun, silent, and powerful in its silence. It rested on a tree branch not more than twenty meters away, and regarded me. I regarded him in return. I had known for years there are owls in the area: I've heard their hooting, and seen their pellets on the ground. But until that day and for ten years, I hadn't seen one here before. Further, and I think importantly, since I had entered the forest that day for no particular purpose but to enjoy a warm autumn afternoon, to reaffirm my love for the park's landmarks and vistas, and to experience a few hours of pure human freedom, in simpler words *to play*, the encounter with the owl could take on a magical meaning. In the light of such magic, what a magnificent animal he was! How proud he seemed, as though in charge of the world, as though I required his permission to take another step. How *unpretentious*, too: this owl had no need to pretend to be something he was not. The size of his claws, the laser-focus of his eyes meeting mine, was proof enough that he was a predator.

No need to flex his weapons or to brandish them. And what a delightful conversation we might have, if he were to speak. How much he could tell of the places he had seen, the adventures he had while hunting, and the pleasure of flight. Much as I would have loved to stay and hear him speak, I decided to move on after a few minutes. I did not know whether meeting his eyes might be provocative. And much as I might enjoy telling the story of how I got owl-claw scars on my face, I certainly would not enjoy getting them. In ten years I've seen hundreds of species of animals in the forest: white-tailed deer; almost close enough that I could touch them; snakes underfoot causing me to jump with surprise; hummingbirds pooping on my shoulder. That same autumn, I encountered a bear: another magnificent animal, and one much more likely to kill me if I stayed nearby for too long. Yet nothing stands out in my mind quite as strong as that silent conversation with the owl. Such is the magic of the forest. It can mean what you want it to mean under the aspect of play, yet at the same time it can surprise, and threaten, and *reveal* itself, in ways no human artifact can do. It can suggest a kind of magic no human artifact can adopt: the dramatic discovery of a world not made by human hands. Thus it participates in the play, bringing its own contribution to the emergence of meaning. Perhaps this spring I will be surprised by a new meltwater pond, or a patch of flowers growing in a new place, or a pair of rabbits dashing out of the shrubbery as my footsteps startle them. That, too, will be a dramatic discovery; that, too, will be magical.

The good news is that this kind of play, though it comes easiest to children, remains available to all. No one loses the ability to play so long as they continue playing. The bad news is that your magic sword needs to be kept sharp; it has a tendency to go dull from lack of adventure. The magical lives of children, particularly as seen in role-play and pretending, tends to decline rather quickly after a child's preschool years.[156] It declines for reasons that I think deserve a meditation of their own.

But let me conclude this meditation with a fourth answer to the first of my root questions. What human reality emerges from the encounter with the earth? *A sense of the boundaries of the human world; and beyond those boundaries, a sense of possibilities for play, dramatic discovery, and magic; possibilities that are not available within the boundaries of the human world.*

Adolescence: Disenchantment

In most of my formative years I did not have many friends, and I did not want many friends. I had my forest, and I had my bedroom with its Lego collection and its treasury of books, and I had my mind. Most of the time, these were enough for me. But somewhere in my mid-teens, I contracted a condition that is perhaps common for people of that age: *disenchantment.* This word normally denotes the condition of one who lost their innocence. In my view, disenchantment is the condition of one who dwells in a narrow and limited world, consisting entirely or almost entirely of interests that are personal in nature and which are fulfilled or realised entirely or almost entirely within a human field of life: the fields of society, culture, politics, economics, families, and interpersonal relations. Disenchantment is not so much a loss of magic, but a re-direction of one's attention away from the wider world of nature and cosmos, and toward a more limited human world. A disenchanted person, as I shall define them, lives in the world of the human, perhaps only in their own personal world, and does not step out of it. A disenchanted world assigns no special qualities to meadows, or rivers, or stars. And regardless of whether your childhood included such things, as mine did, still there are certain events and forces which occur in adolescence that work to enclose you within the realm of the human, and to exclude intrusions from the realms of land and sea and sky. These are the events and forces of disenchantment.

In our culture today the word *disenchantment* tends to have the connotation of loss, and sorrow because of loss. This has deep roots in Western culture, coming from assumed mythologies about the idyllic life enjoyed by Adam and Eve, before the Fall, as well as romantic philosophies that glamorize the Golden Ages of Greece or Rome, the innocence of childhood, and the corrupting influence of civilization. The sociologist Max Weber announced in *The Protestant Work Ethic and the Spirit of Capitalism* (1905) that the magic of the world had been banished from modern life, first of all by Puritan Christianity, and then by industrialization and scientific rationalism.[157] Numerous social researchers responding to him sought to prove either that he was wrong, or that the process of disenchantment could be reversed.[158] Well, perhaps. But I'd like to take a more personal view here. Disenchantment, as I see it, emerges from certain kinds of encounters with the immensities of Loneliness, and of Other People: especially those encounters which confront the individual with *transience*, *injustice*, and *boundaries*. That is to say: the discoveries of things emerging from the future and fading into the past, of things given and taken without fairness, and of things which once seemed free but which became either denied or else shuttered behind a paywall. These experiences don't emerge from historical forces or cultural changes, as Weber's argument claimed. They emerge, rather, from growing up.

Children's literature seems to understand this point remarkably well. A.A. Milne, the author of the beloved Winnie The Pooh novels, included just such an observation in *The House At Pooh Corner* (1928), the last novel in the series. Near the end of the story, Christopher Robin attempted to explain to an uncomprehending Pooh that he was being sent to a boarding school, and he would no longer be able to visit the Hundred Acre Wood:

> Suddenly Christopher Robin began to tell Pooh about some of the things: People called Kings and Queens and something called Factors, and a place called Europe, and an island in the

middle of the sea where no ships came, and how you make a Suction Pump (if you want to), and when Knights were Knighted, and what comes from Brazil. And Pooh, his back against one of the sixty-something trees and his paws folded in front of him, said "Oh!" and "I didn't know," and thought how wonderful it would be to have a Real Brain which could tell you things. And by-and-by Christopher Robin came to an end of the things, and was silent, and he sat there looking out over the world, and wishing it wouldn't stop...

Then, suddenly again, Christopher Robin, who was still looking at the world, with his chin in his hands, called out "Pooh!"

"Yes?" said Pooh.

"When I'm –when –Pooh!"

"Yes, Christopher Robin?"

"I'm not going to do Nothing any more."

"Never again?"

"Well, not so much. They don't let you."[159]

As I entered my teens and my high-school years, that moment in Christopher Robin's life cast itself into much sharper meaning for me. Childhood fantasies of mine that once seemed real, not only to me but also to some of my friends, were captured behind the locked doors of adult expectations. After a certain double-digit birthday, no one wanted to be an astronaut anymore, no one wanted to explore forests in search of faeries, no one imagined that they had come to earth from the stars. No one thought it natural anymore to sing happy songs out loud when they were happy or sad songs when they were sad: such behaviour now elicited from peers and adults a puzzled and judgmental stare. Where once the priest read to my class the Biblical quotations about the goodness of childhood, now he read quotations about growing up: "When I became a man, I put the ways of childhood behind me." (1 Corinthians 13:11). I learned from these stern events that I was no longer permitted to be who I was, and that I was obliged to become someone else. I could define that new identity for myself only so long as its broadest contours remained within acceptable bounds. This was not only something adults taught me: other boys of about the same age cheerfully imposed the same lesson on me as well as on each other. One of them, S.B., who was one year ahead of me in school, told me that Depeche Mode and New Order was the music of the future, and that listening to them was obligatory. Another boy, T.M., stole a wooden coin bank that I had made in woodworking class, and got an excellent grade for it: when I told the teacher what happened, he didn't believe me. That same boy also decided that I was queer. I didn't know at the time that the word was code for a boy who is sexually oriented to other boys: I only knew, from all the social-contextual signs, that it was bad to be queer. In fact, I discovered an interest in girls at that age. But I also discovered no girls in my class were interested in me. My forest was still my refuge and my sanctuary, but I was coming to grasp that it would not be so forever. More tourists were coming to see it, bringing with them more noise, and leaving behind more garbage. A fence was erected along the edge of the gorge, with bright yellow signs to warn people of the danger – the danger of the self-same geographic wonder that the tourists had come to see. I also knew a time would arrive, perhaps after high school, when I would have to leave my village to find a job and pay rent. In short, I would have to leave my forest and live in the human world more or less full time. I was no longer permitted to do Nothing. And in that human world, things pass away, things are unfair, time is regulated and scheduled, and things are unavailable or inaccessible, sometimes pending a gatekeeper fee, sometimes permanently. The forest would no longer be a daily experience in my life. The meanings of the things and places around me could no longer emerge from play: they now came from other people's demands and expectations.

Thus the places, activities, and anticipations of childhood were falling behind me, or stripped from me, as I rafted along a slow-flowing yet unstoppable river into an unmapped future.

No specific social movements or forces need to be blamed for the disenchantment that arises from growing up, although any number of them can contribute. Rather, disenchantment is in some way bound into the biologically-inevitable process of leaving childhood behind and entering adulthood. For as you grow into adolescence, your body takes on properties unseen in childhood which makes it a potential instrument for other people's interests: its strength for physical labour, its brain-complexity for problem-solving or managerial tasks, its readiness for conceiving and bearing children. Growing into adolescence means taking on a new significance for others, whether you like it or not. (Women know this better than men. As a girl's body takes on a more mature shape, older men take new interest in them, often unwelcome and intrusive interest.) And with this new significance comes new forms of interaction, new expectations, and new demands. From these new interactions emerges the consciousness of transience, injustice, and boundaries: the trio of experiences which reduces the freedom and ability to play, and thereby leaves us with a life less magical.

Upon realising that your life has been disenchanted, what remains? *A life in a world of mere objects and facts about objects; a life where all values in the surrounding world are instrumental values.* This serves as a fifth answer to my root question. And while a world of objects may have interesting properties and relations, their value can only be instrumental, utilitarian, or nothing. Without magic, so it may seem, they can possess no *intrinsic* meaning.

Adulthood: Work And Mastery

You're an adult now. You're old enough to vote, to sit on juries, to join the army, to buy a house. You can do anything you like, so long as you have a job that pays you enough to do it, and so long as you don't hurt anyone (or as long as you don't get caught). Let's suppose that you have a steady job, some nice clothes, enough food, a phone, a bank account, and an internet connection. Perhaps you live with your partner, and you share a car and a home in a safe and clean neighbourhood. Perhaps you go camping in the summer, and perhaps you go to the movies or to pubs and restaurants with friends as often as you can.

As for me, in my early adulthood, I'm in my grandfather's forest. Every February for most of my twenties, my cousin J.F. and I would join my grandparents to help them tap the sugar maples. We young bucks drilled holes in the trees with a petrol-powered drill. Then Grandad hammered a spigot into the hole and attached it to a rubber hose, to lead the syrup to the sugar shack. By the end of the week, the whole forest was networked with hoses. The sap would pour out of the end of the network as fast as a kitchen sink, even before we powered up the pump. Sometimes we would attach the hoses to long lengths of galvanized wire, to keep them on the correct angle for gravity to pull the sap down to the sugar shack. These wires had to be tightened with a winch-like device, and we often had to balance on top of a long ladder to do it. It was hard, heavy, and sometimes dangerous work. In temperatures of minus 5 degrees Celsius we could sweat enough to drop our coats and work in our shirt-sleeves. Then we four, my cousin, my grandparents, and I, ate a dinner big enough to feed a platoon, and slept as deep as the dead. And we loved it.

My grandfather was a farmer for much of his life. He was also a school teacher and a Boy Scout leader; he loved to introduce young people to the forest. He loved the land. Let no one have any doubts about that. The point I want to emphasize here is the way in which my intentions, on going into the forest to help him to tap the trees, changed my perception of the trees. The *value* of the forest, at least while I was working there, became a matter of its *usefulness* for my grandfather's purposes. That, by itself, did not make the old magic disappear. But it did make the old magic wane away, a little. Instead of looking for sinkholes that were good for hide-and-seek, or looking for sticks to make swords and fortress-posts, I had to keep in mind the property boundary with the neighbour's farm, and how close the tractor path was to the tree I was chopping or drilling, and whether a certain tree had been tapped last year and where to tap it this year. None of those facts were new to me. But they had little meaning under the aspect of play. Under the aspect of work, they held much greater meaning. Work is the polar opposite of *play*, and thus it has a disenchanting effect on things: both on the forest, and on me.

Most of the time, we do not see objects in the world in terms of their objective properties. We see them, instead, in terms of their values and meanings in relation to our intentions. You may have heard this idea expressed in the famous aphorism, "we do not see things as they are: we see them as we are."[160] Or in this one: "...it is tempting, if the only tool you have is a hammer, to treat everything as if it were a nail."[161] Philosophically, the basic idea, though not the exact phrase, goes back to Edmund Husserl,[162] the father of a branch of philosophy called phenomenology. I would like to examine some implications of this idea which illuminate the tension between our being-ecological and our being-free.

Having the intention to go to the forest, not to play but to work, the forest and all its life appears to us not in its own terms, but rather in terms of the values and meanings of whatever work you had gone there to do. Thus, under the aspect of work, the earth and all its materials and life-forms appear to be:

1. *Available*: they can be inspected, evaluated, harvested, gathered, and stockpiled.
2. *Useful*: upon inspecting the things of earth, some will appear to be useful for the work we're doing, perhaps as raw materials or perhaps as tools. Some things will appear as indispensable necessities and others as options. If a

thing of earth appears to have none of these values, then it will appear either as an obstacle or as an irrelevance.

3. *Malleable*: the things of earth can be worked upon, modified, purified, purged out, changed up, switched around, transformed, chopped apart, joined together, and disposed – even at the level of its molecules and atoms – by inputs of human labour. A dozen tree trunks becomes a cord of firewood; a long straight trunk becomes a stack of lumber, which in turn becomes a table, a chair, a desk, a window frame.

4. *Possessable*: it is possible to treat the things of earth as foundation-markers for a regime of legal estate. To put it another way, they can be transformed into the substrate of a hyper-reality of private property, trade and sale value, taxable wealth, and legal regulation. Thus, a mass of material becomes a consumer 'good' that belongs to, and is proper to, somebody somewhere; that's why we call it 'property'. A dozen tree trunks becomes, not merely a cord of firewood, but *my grandfather's* firewood. A master-crafted writing desk becomes not just any desk, but *my* desk.

5. *Displayable*: that hyper-reality of property-ownership can be equally as satisfying, to many people if not to everyone, as the work of taking up the things of earth and turning them into consumer goods, for the reason that the hyper-reality of legal estate is easier to show off to others. The products of the earth, in combination with the hyper-real regime of legal estate, can become *bids for social recognition and public prestige*, recognizable by anyone including those who have no grasp of the use-value or the malleability of the materials.

6. *Infinitely renewable:* as per the illusion of infinite carrying capacity.

Is there no other way for things to appear? Can things possess no other values besides being useful, necessary, an obstacle, or an irrelevance? Or is there a way to find magic in the things of earth even under the aspect of work? I think perhaps there can be, if we consider a very old and strange concept in phenomenology: the concept of *aletheia*: 'un-hiddenness', 'un-forgotten', 'disclosed', 'unconcealed', 'revealing'.

To explain it: the *malleability* of the things of earth makes them appear to us, under the aspect of work, as raw materials. And as raw materials they are potentially many different kinds of finished products. To manufacture something from those materials is also to *reveal* one of those potentials. The carving-chisel reveals the statue of David hidden deep inside the marble. The digger reveals the coal behind the face of the coal mine. The logger reveals the lumber in the tree, and the carpenter reveals the furniture in the lumber. Work, even while having the very opposite character of play, can thus take on at least *some* of the character of magic. From out of a mass of raw materials, a craftsperson conjured up a finished product. The craftsperson's skill, experience, training, erudition, perceptual intelligence, and various choices, as well as standards of excellence bequeathed to us by various traditions, supplies much of the sense of magic here.[163] To someone who does not possess those professional skills, the creation of a bookshelf out of a heap of wooden planks can look like magic, feel like magic. It is as if the bookshelf has been revealed to us from behind a magician's curtain, or as if it has arrived here after a journey from another world. *Aletheia* is a name for what it feels like to witness that revealing. It is a word for the occasion when we realize – when we *make real,* when we bring to reality – some potential that may have lain dormant within something all along, beyond the horizon of the unseen.

As should be obvious, the same *aletheia* can appear in natural events. It is in the grass and the soil emerging from under the melting spring snow. It is in the opening of flowers, the hatching of birds from their eggs, the welling-up of water from a spring, the sunrise in the morning, the stars coming out at twilight, the waxing of the moon. Precisely this action, a natural value emerging from out of the hidden and into the light, makes a forest into a magic forest: a realm of discovery and play wider than that which can be found in the human world. A previous answer to my second root question finds new confirmation.

But under the aspect of work, human agency *is* involved. For it is not any random force that transformed a forest into a stockpile of lumber, and transformed a stockpile of lumber into a house. Rather, it is someone's labour. And from this combination of *aletheia* and *agency* comes a sense of *power:* a sense of that some state of affairs in the world is a product of your will, a product of your design. From this sense of power can arise new feelings of potential, new realities within us that could be revealed by new acts of will. Indeed, the will to power becomes the most prominent part of human being-free. On seeing what you have done, what else could one do? On seeing what you have taken, what else can you take? What other things could be made from the things of earth? And what proper pride might we earn by making them?

Answers to such questions were seen all too clearly by the philosopher Martin Heidegger, and they bring us to a very dark place. *Aletheia*, he says, is the essence of technology:

> Instrumentality is considered to be the fundamental characteristic of technology. If we inquire step by step into what technology, represented as means [ie. instrumentality], actually is, then we shall arrive at revealing [*aletheia*]. The possibility of all productive manufacture lies in revealing... if we give heed to this, then another whole realm for the essence of technology will open itself up to us. It is the realm of revealing, ie. of truth.[164]

Earth Spirit: The Circle of Life is Broken

Aletheia, 'revealing', combined with the human force of agency, can make some people feel as if the earth has called upon them to take it, claim it, work upon it, and possess it. Heidegger says: "...man in the technological age is, in a particularly striking way, challenged forth into revealing... Always the destining [the inevitability] of revealing [*aletheia*] holds sway over man."[165] An echo of the first chapter of Genesis can be heard here: Adam and Eve, the progenitors of humanity, are commanded by God to "Be fruitful and increase in number; fill the earth and subdue it. Rule over the fish in the sea and the birds in the sky and over every living creature that moves on the ground." (Gen. 1:28). We are, Heidegger says, compelled and called-upon to rule the Earth; one might say we are trapped in the position of having to rule it. And yet the will to *aletheia* is, for Heidegger, a kind of freedom, a kind of ultimate expression of the human spirit: "Freedom is the realm of the destining that at any given time starts a revealing upon its way."[166]

That confirmation of the will to power over the Earth is dark enough. But another, deeper darkness appears when Heidegger draws the conclusion from this argument: that under the aspect of work we may find ourselves treating *everything*, all the things of earth, all its materials and all its life, *including other human beings*, as raw materials. And we may find ourselves unable to see things any other way:

> As soon as what is unconcealed no longer concerns man even as object, but does so, rather, exclusively as standing-reserve... then he comes to the very brink of a precipitous fall; that is, he comes to the point where *he himself will have to be taken as standing-reserve*. Meanwhile man, precisely as the one so threatened, exalts himself to the posture of lord of the earth.[167]

Thus Heidegger warns that technology treats human beings as

120

raw materials for some powerful person's application of will: human beings, under the aspect of work, become available, useful, malleable, and possessable, no less than the trees and stones of a forest.

Yet Heidegger makes a distinction between traditional technology and *modern* technology. Traditional technology, as he describes it, cooperates with the forces of nature. "The work of the peasant does not challenge the soil of the field. In sowing grain it places seed in the keeping of the forces of growth and watches over its increase." A romantic notion of pre-modern agriculture, to be sure; but it sets up his point about modern technology, which *"sets upon* nature... in the sense of *challenging* it. Agriculture is now the mechanized food industry. Air is now *set upon* to yield nitrogen, the earth to yield ore, ore to yield uranium..."[168] (Notice the language of predatory conquest here: the things-of-earth are "challenged" and "set upon", like a fighter attacking an opponent.) Furthermore: while traditional technology gathers the things-of-earth to meet the immediate needs of the craftsperson herself and her associates, modern technology gathers everything it can, far beyond immediate needs, to collect them in *a standing-reserve,* ready and waiting for future needs:

> Everywhere everything is ordered to stand by, to be immediately on hand, indeed to stand there just so that it may be on call for a further ordering. Whatever is ordered about in this way has its own standing. We call it the standing-reserve [*Bestand*].[169]

It's modern technology, not traditional technology, which Heidegger says treats people and the things-of-earth alike as raw materials. Traditional technology, he says, is more like *poesis,* 'poetry': "There was a time when the bringing-forth of the true into the beautiful was called *techne*. The *poesis* of the fine arts was also called *techne*."[170]

Something like this, perhaps, is what people in technology-intensive urbanized societies mean when they express a wish for a simpler life, a more 'authentic' life. They want a life where, as Heidegger quotes the poet Holderlin, "poetically man dwells upon the earth." It is a wish that also appeals to me. I, too, want hand-crafted furniture, locally grown food, houses whose materials and designs fit with local landscapes and climates, locally made decorative arts, and meaningful work to produce such things for myself and my community. I, too, want to hear bird song outside my windows, and wind in the trees, instead of car engines and sirens. I, too, want tallgrass fields to walk in, hills to climb, and stars at night to contemplate. I, too, want a life where work and technology is applied for the sake of simple pleasures, and where I am not a unit in anyone's standing reserve.

But Heidegger's argument about traditional technology is not an effective counter-argument to the conclusion I drew above: that under the aspect of work, the things-of-earth, and eventually human beings themselves, possess only utilitarian value. For the nature of traditional work still empties the things-of-earth of their own *aletheia,* and transfers it to carpenters, potters, stonemasons, tailors and seamstresses, bookbinders, winemakers, gardeners and farmers, labourers and craftspeople of all kinds, musicians and artists too. The products of such people's work can be magical in their own way, as we have seen. But in the course of this transfer, the *aletheia* of the earth is humanized, enclosed within the human world: Heidegger uses the word 'enframing', to dramatize how the things-of-earth are captured into an ever-expanding human realm. Under the aspect of traditional work, you might still speak of a tree as beautiful; but its beauty would be in the discovery that it is more conspicuously useful than expected, or that its wood can contribute to the manufacture of a product of unusually high quality. Under the aspect of work, there are no other categories of value. If you want to find the original *aletheia* of the tree that someone cut down to build a house, you have to let go of the aspect of work, and look upon the house some other way.

With all that said, let us state the sixth answer to the root question 'what becomes of the human reality, etc.': *a sense of confidence, privilege, and entitlement, to be master and possessor of the earth and all its values.*

Adulthood: Shifting Baselines

Humanity is not the only species whose participation in the ecosystem is global. We are, however, the species causing the *most* global ecological change *right now*. In that respect, we could view the climate crisis as merely the latest stage in a four-billion-year-old history of global ecological succession. But we are driving the kind of succession that will, if allowed to continue, render large areas of the Earth unfit for most forms of animal life, including human life. Temperature is the easiest sign of this change to measure and to communicate. By taking measurements from ice cores, sea sediments, tree-ring measurements, and so on, scientists estimate that the average temperature of Earth's northern hemisphere was mostly stable until about the middle decades of the 20th century, when it rose up about 0.2 degrees per decade.[171] Our industrial greenhouse gasses may warm the earth into a state that's hotter than the human body can handle, and hotter than the temperature-niche of many of the animals and plants we rely on for food. That's what makes it not just a change, but a crisis.

But most people don't see it. To explain why, I think it is not enough to say that most people live in terms of an anthropocentric worldview, or that they are disenchanted, or something similar. Rather, I think we need the help of another principle of ecology: *shifting baseline syndrome.*

To explain: The reference points for what counts as 'healthy' or 'normal' in the environment, including the reference points followed by the most committed environmental campaigners, are seeded into our consciousness from a very early age. But ecosystems are always changing. A given ecosystem might take many decades, even a century or two, to change from one state to another. Most human lives, however, are not lived on that kind of time scale. Let's say that a human time scale is the same as the average length of a human life in an affluent country and in the early twenty-first century: that's about 75 years. That's plenty of time to witness a fair amount of ecological change: riverbank erosions, a season that arrives earlier or later, a summer with more storms than last, a winter with heavier snow. But it's not enough time to witness a whole-scale global process of ecological succession. The result is that you are predisposed to imagine that the state of things when you were a child is the way things have always been. You'll assume the Earth's temperature range, its abundance and diversity of wildlife, the shape and age of forests, the distribution of farmland to bush to wilderness, and so on, such as it was through your childhood and early adulthood, is the way it had always been throughout history. Thus, most of the environmental changes you happen to notice in your lifetime are likely to be rather slight, subtle, and unimportant. You're noticing them on the human scale, where they appear to be not much to worry about. But by the time your children or your grandchildren reach adulthood, the ecology will have changed a little, and they will think that the new state of things is the way things have always been. Each human generation will live with a different idea of what counts as the natural and healthy 'baseline' of the concept's name. As a result, we fail to notice changes playing out on longer timelines, or we fail to grasp their significance.

It is this combination of ecosystem succession and shifting baseline syndrome, which I think explains humanity's failure to act on the climate crisis, not a fault in our worldviews or in our thinking. In order to grasp the full scale of the climate crisis, we need to think beyond the human scale of time: something even the most imaginative and intelligent people among us find hard to do. From this observation, I think we can draw the following insight: *we do not know, from personal experience, what a 'normal' and 'healthy' state for the global biosphere looks like.* It is even possible that there is no 'normal' or 'healthy' state for the Earth. There are, perhaps, various 'climax' states in which the biosphere maximizes its capacity for biodiversity, biomass, and energy discharge, at least for a while. But those climax states need not be any particular type of biome (ie. a forest, a grassland, a jungle, etc.); and they may or may not be a state that we human beings can live in.

The most important fact that we have missed as a result of shifting baseline syndrome is not the climate crisis. Rather, it's the fact that over centuries of civilization, and especially since the advent of industrialization, we human beings have become no longer one mammalian species among many. We are now a force of nature in our own right. Hitherto I have considered the *individual* human being encountering the Earth in various ways. But my grandfather and I are not the only people in the forest chopping wood. All over the world, millions of people are cutting trees from their forests to build houses, heat them in the cold, and create all the things we create using wood. All over the world, armies of woodcutters, miners, fishing crews, oil and gas riggers, farmers, surveyors, and prospectors, 'set upon' and 'challenge' the Earth to give up its treasures. Most of these are organized in regiments called corporations and armed with heavy machinery. The aggregate of all this work is a global force, affecting a large range of ecosystem indicators and functions. Temperature, ocean acidity, cloud cover, planetary albedo, the soil microbiome, the water cycle, the chemical makeup of the atmosphere, the size and shape of deserts, and so on, are all pushed and pulled by the Leviathan-strength of humanity's many arms. Nor is this a new observation. As early as the nineteenth century, some scientists saw that the steam engine and the blast furnace, the two cornerstone technologies of the first Industrial Revolution, could change the chemical composition of the atmosphere. G.P. Marsh published *The Earth As Modified By Human Action* in 1864; Antonio Stoppani wrote in 1873 that humankind was a "new telluric force which in power and universality may be compared to the greater forces of earth." Today scientists tend to use the word for this global force coined by scientists Paul Crutzen and Eugene Stoermer: *the Anthropocene.* Here's what Crutzen said of it:

> For the past three centuries, the effects of humans on the global environment have escalated. Because of these anthropogenic emissions of carbon dioxide, global climate may depart significantly from natural behaviour for many millennia to come. It seems appropriate to assign the term 'Anthropocene' to the present, in many ways human-dominated, geological epoch, supplementing the Holocene – the warm period of the past 10–12 millennia. The Anthropocene could be said to have started in the latter part of the eighteenth century, when analyses of air trapped in polar ice showed the beginning of growing global concentrations of carbon dioxide and methane. This date also happens to coincide with James Watt's design of the steam engine in 1784.[172]

To say we live in the Anthropocene is a way of saying we now live in a period of history where almost no part of the planet is untouched by humanity. Whether by harvesting materials and energy, or by leaving our waste behind, everything on Earth feels our footprints. Today, fifty-one million square kilometres, or roughly one-half of all the habitable land-surface of the Earth, is farmland or related agricultural.[173] A thousand years ago, that figure was only four million square kilometres.[174] Since the end of the last Ice Age, we have cleared one-third of the Earth's forests away.[175] The majority of that forest destruction happened between the years 1920 and 1980: we destroyed around 115 million hectares per decade in that period, four times the rate of deforestation for the previous hundred years. In the 1980s, we destroyed 151 million hectares globally.[176] In places where we don't farm or don't build cities, 'barren lands' like the upland heaths of England, the deserts of the Levant, and the plains of Iceland, our footprint can still be felt: such lands are what they are because of thousands of years of tree-felling and livestock farming, going all the way back to the Neolithic age.[177] There are, of course, landscapes on the Earth with no human settlements and no farms, neither historically nor today. But even in those areas, the chemical composition of the air and of the precipitation is tinted and toned by our pollution. And finally, we find the footprint of civilization inside our bodies: scientists estimated that every human being on earth has microplastics, nanometer-sized particles of plastic, inside our cells.[178] Thus humanity's footprint presses itself everywhere, leaving nothing unstamped, nothing untrodden. But the walking pace of humanity is measured on the scale of civilizations and historical epochs – a scale beyond the human, even while it emerges from the human. And so, we don't notice.

Putting these three concepts together – ecological succession, shifting baseline, and the Anthropocene, we can draw a seventh answer to the root question 'what becomes of the human reality, etc.': *a state of ignorance concerning what counts as healthy or normal in the environment; a state of ignorance concerning what an untampered, truly wild, truly 'natural' environment actually looks like, if ever there was such a thing; a state of ignorance concerning what a sustainable, symbiotic, and truly cooperative relationship with the Earth can be.*

Middle Age: The Urban Hyper-Reality

Let's imagine you're in middle age now. You're not yet old but no longer young. You're still strong, quick, energetic, ambitious, and capable. You can still do everything you enjoyed doing in your twenties. But now it takes longer to recover. You've gained more life experience and built up more life history, and thus you have a stronger grasp of who you are. With that stronger sense of self comes a clarified picture of what you want in life. You know what gives you lasting happiness, and what doesn't. You know the consequences of foolish choices. You are more resilient under stress and tragedy. It's more difficult for fashion and peer pressure to move you; the judgmental gaze of other people has less power. You still have the imagination and adventurousness of your youth, but less energy for it: perhaps because the dreams of your youth have proven to be unreachable, or perhaps you did reach them but found them unsatisfying anyway. You also have less time for youthful adventure: you have responsibilities to your job, your children, your pets, your property if you are a homeowner, and so on. And besides that: being middle aged now, you need more sleep. Where once you and your friends spoke of changing the world, now you speak of changing your internet provider.

A few years ago, I myself reached middle age. I looked at my life and realized: *This is it*. What I have now is what I get for the rest of my life. I have a partner and we have a loving relationship. I have a good job, a fine home, and a few good friends. I am in good health, and I have a few small accomplishments that bring me proper pride. This is what all the choices I've made and all the work I've done has led to. Barring anything unexpected (a global pandemic, perhaps?), I can say that my future looks good. But the point to emphasize here is that my future is no longer quite as "open", "free", "full of potential", as it seemed when I was younger. I am still a human being-free, but my life is now strongly configured by the choices I made over the years, and all the forces set in motion by their consequences.

In a similar fashion, the relation between Earth and humanity is also middle-aged. Thousands of years of civilization now lie behind us: we today inherit more than three million years of it, counting back to the approximate beginnings of human art, science, technology, and culture, in the Paleolithic age. We grew from 1.8 billion people in 1921, the year my grandfather was born, to 7.8 billion people in the year my grandfather turns a century. For most of human history, including up to the year 1800, the majority of humanity lived in villages and small towns. Around the year 2017, more than half of us lived in a city, for the first time in human history.[179] At the turn of the millennium, only twenty-one years previous to the day I write these words, there were 371 cities in the world with a million or more inhabitants. In 2018, only three years ago, there were 548 cities with a million people. Thirty-three of these are megacities: urban areas with more than ten million people.[180]

For those who live in the city, everything is humanized; everything incarnates the spirit of our being-free. Nothing, not even a forest park or a garden, is innocent of human influence. Even the trees are subject to zoning plans, bylaws, selection committees, and designs. Geometric forms dominate the view: straight lines, right angles, smooth curves, arithmetic proportions, and regular symmetries inform the buildings and road grids, often measured within millimetres of Platonic perfection. Thus the urban world comes more closely to resemble the workings of the intellect; the realm of the mind. Synthetic materials like glass, concrete, and steel, fill these forms. Especially in the core of a modern city, hardly any organic materials or shapes are in sight. Meandering lines, broken symmetries, clay, wood, and unpolished stone, when they appear, emerge from a designer's decision to subvert the geometric rationality of humanized spaces: they serve as exceptions to prove the rule. Electric light, in people's homes and in public streets, in billboards and neon signage, eradicate all natural darkness. Clocks in our watches, phones, computers, cars, kitchen appliances, and bedside tables, allows us to ignore the rising and the setting of the sun. Together, our clocks and our electric lights capture and humanize time itself. Space, too, has been domesticated: not only by geometry, but by transportation technology. The fossil fuel engines in our cars, aircraft, and boats, allow us to travel faster than natural wind, water, or muscle power could carry us. Some cities are deliberately designed to discourage that most natural form of transport, *walking,* by building most of its public commons into car-friendly and pedestrian-unfriendly roads and parking lots. Some facilities like markets, airports, government buildings, concert halls, and businesses cannot be visited on foot at all, or else with increasing danger.

There are some who regard the creation of the urban hyper-reality as a clear benefit to humanity. Perhaps there is something wonderful, even glorious, in humanity's technological power. We elevate ourselves, we push back the limitations imposed on us, we expand our degrees of freedom, when we test our intelligence and our strength against the forces of nature. An hydro-electric dam is an example of humanity turning our collective knowledge and will into a force equally as powerful as nature, if not more so; a force capable of diverting or stopping the flow of a magnificent river. If nature is a god, in the sense of a power beyond the capacity of humanity to resist or even to understand, then a hydroelectric dam is *a power to rival the gods.* Or to be less hyperbolic: with science and technology we elevate ourselves to new dimensions of being-free, above and beyond the limitations of nature which in the mythopoetic past seemed insurmountable.

Architects and engineers are often keen to frame this point in spiritual terms – that is to say, in terms of humanity's collective will to power and to self-creation. "Every machine is a spiritualization of an organism," wrote the Dutch architect Theo Van Doesburg. "The machine is, par excellence, a phenomenon of spiritual discipline."[181] Architect Bruno Taut wrote: "The direct carrier of the spiritual forces, moulder of the sensibilities of the general public, which today are slumbering and tomorrow will awake, is architecture."[182] Philosopher Karsten Harries, who has perhaps done the most to articulate the philosophical dimensions of architecture, wrote that architecture's process of appropriating and humanizing the world is a function of the human spirit:

> History is the progress of such appropriation, where art and architecture are part of the effort to make the natural and sensible our own, to rob it of its character of being a mute, alien other and thus to transform it into a dwelling place fit for human beings. To carve a statue, to build a pyramid is to humanize nature, to breathe spirit into matter.[183]

Understood in terms like these, the Industrial Revolution, when we transitioned from wind, water, and animal power, to coal, steam, and electricity, was a kind of spiritual revolution. All the modern realities we take for granted today because of that revolution could be treated as measurements of how far we have escaped the confines of our being-ecological, and migrated into ever-deeper and ever-wider degrees of being-free, where we may express our spirit more openly and more completely.

But we have hardly noticed this move. For one reason, as we have seen, the baseline of what counts as 'normal' in the environment shifts with every generation. For another: at least in the most technologically intensive and advanced societies, no one actually looks at or listens to their material environments anymore. Instead we attend to *media-transmitted representations* of our environments, captured by cameras and microphones or else generated in computers, selected and curated by artificially-intelligent algorithms for maximum addictive effect, visually edited for colour and proportion, and displayed on digital screens. Almost all knowledge, including knowledge about one's own city, comes from images, sound-bites, catch-phrases, headlines, and memes, all of them electronically transmitted.

They come at us fast, like the surprise attack of an army invading your mind, and yet they disappear just as fast: consigned to irrelevance in the span of a news cycle, or even at the click of the 'Refresh' button mere seconds after arrival. We moderns have come to prefer images, representations, and satirical-ironic depreciations of reality, over direct unmediated experience. While there has always been escapism in storytelling, never before has there been a global fantasy-industrial complex of film and television studios, social media, streaming video services, online influencers, photo-editing apps on smartphones, immersive computer role-play games, and the like, where people may attend to synthesized artificial realities for the majority of their waking hours. The meagre fragments of the World of Earth that remain – a patch of grass breaking through the asphalt, for instance, or a city park that requires a bus or a car to reach – cannot compete for our attention.

Nor is this limited to entertainment. In the forums of social media, where a majority of people now read of news that might inform their civic and political engagements, algorithms weaponize people's values against them, by showing each user a never-ending stream of validating comfort-messages and anger-inducing threat-messages, all to keep you attending to the forum instead of to your life – indeed to make the forum usurp the place of the physical setting of your life, as exemplified by the saying "I'm a digital native, I live my life online". The algorithms nudge these messages over time toward increasingly radical and puritanical positions, leading us to commit ourselves to deeper dimensions of self-righteousness and outrage, and to limit our friends to those with the same puritanical commitments: *incipit* the echo chamber and the epistemic silo. This leaves everyone's minds beholden to the owners and controllers of the means of mass communication, and the algorithms that manage them: less able to know, and thus less able to speak of, or even to think about, anything that the fantasy-industrial complex cannot or will not transmit. And even when we develop a healthy capacity for media literacy and reasonable doubt: everything is framed by sales pitches and corporate sponsors.

In sum: we created an *urban hyper-reality* of Platonic geometry, synthetic materials, thermodynamic machine-powered labour, immersive media fantasy, echo chambers, and epistemic silos, detached both physically and psychologically from the organic messiness of our being-ecological as far as the technology will allow, funded by advertisers and consumer subscriptions, and valued higher than our being-ecological by a majority of people. The urban hyper-reality is, in its own way, an immensity. It stands beyond any individual human being's ability to grasp, and it configures our lives and our realities through the choices we make in response to it. I'm not passing judgment upon it here: I'm only pointing out that it exists. *This is it.* This is the world as we have made it. This is the logical product of three million years of work and mastery, let loose upon a disenchanted Earth.

Thus we come into possession of an eighth answer to my root question. What human reality emerges from the encounter with the Earth? *None. For we are no longer looking at the Earth, no longer listening to her. We are responding to different immensities.*

But as a brief addendum: if we do not face the Earth, if we remain immersed in the urban hyper-real, then we will continue to take the Earth for granted, and we will never overcome the illusion of infinite carrying capacity. And the climate crisis shall carry on.

Middle Age: No Climate Reckoning

There shall be a climate reckoning on the occasion when the climate crisis reaches a peak of destructive immensity beyond anyone's ability to reasonably doubt it. The important words in that last sentence are 'beyond *anyone's* ability'. The Reckoning will not be the end of the world as such; it will not be the end of humanity. Indeed this event will be clear only in retrospect, since the climate crisis is not a single event but rather a complex of inter-related events, many of them quite small. But at some time in the future there will be an end to complacency, an end to willed ignorance, an end to denial. And then there will be a mobilization: we will get down to the work of surviving what remains of the climate crisis and emerging from it somehow better than before, if we can. Meanwhile, in the time between today and the Reckoning, there will be billions of preventable deaths, billions of preventable species extinctions, billions of preventable ecosystem collapses. We have a situation comparable to the one Gramsci lamented about in his *Prison Notebooks:* "the crisis consists precisely in the fact that the old is dying and the new cannot be born; in this interregnum a great variety of morbid symptoms appear".

Some might say this reckoning has already begun. We have widespread recycling and composting programs in major cities. The fraction of the global electricity supply produced by renewables (solar, wind, and hydro) grew from ~2,500 terawatt hours in the year 2000, to more than 6,000 TWh in 2018.[184] There are numerous popular movements to lobby governments and influence civil society toward acknowledging and acting on the climate crisis: Extinction Rebellion, for example. Green Party candidates regularly get elected in Europe and in Canada. And in the midst of the Wild Ride there have been many international agreements to reduce greenhouse gas emissions, notably the Paris Accord (2016), the Copenhagen Accord (2006), the Rio+20 conference (2012).

But consider the following events which also took place between the years 2000 and 2020:

- Wild fires in Brazil, sub-Saharan Africa especially Angola, Cameron, and Congo, as well as California USA, Alberta Canada, and Australia.
- Hurricane Katrina.

- The collapse of ice shelves in Antarctica, the melting of the Arctic ice cap, and the Greenland ice sheet.[185]
- In mid-2010, a United Nations summit in Aichi, Japan, identified twenty global biodiversity targets for the world to reach. By mid-2020, *none* of those targets had been met.[186]

What is noteworthy about these events for my purpose here is that powerful voices in our society and culture, including politicians, industry leaders, religious leaders, and celebrities, continued to speak and act as if these were all random and natural events. Tragic and sorrowful events, to be sure. But unconnected to any wider pattern. Definitely unconnected to the way we produce energy and consumer goods, or the way we dispose of our waste. And therefore prompting no need to change anything about the way we live.

The managers and executives of the industries that are destroying our planet are perfectly and completely aware of what they are doing. They are also aware of the consequences. But as long as it's profitable for them to do it, and as long as they can insulate themselves from the consequences, they will keep doing it. For example: at a meeting of the Independent Petroleum Association of America, secretly recorded by one of the participants, oil company executives discussed the need to change, not themselves or their industry, but instead to change people's minds and attitudes toward oil and gas. "Climate change," said Dan Haley, president of the Colorado Oil and Gas Association, "is the prism through which everything is being viewed... We have to be comfortable talking about it, talking about how we are part of the solution through natural gas. And again, hitting people with emotions, hitting them where they're – where their heart is."[187] Similarly, Keith McCoy, a lobbyist for Exxon, also caught in a secret recording, told a journalist that the company's support for a national carbon tax was merely a talking point, and not a serious interest. "Did we aggressively fight against some of the science? Yes. Did we hide our science? Absolutely not... Did we join some of these shadow groups to work against some of the early efforts? Yes, that's true."[188]

So long as attitudes like this remain prominent among the powerful, the climate reckoning will not occur.

Furthermore, we have seen how those well-publicised global environmental conferences produced no results. This is by design, not by accident. The text of the Paris Accord and the Copenhagen Accord commits the signatory nations to nothing, because all of its targets were non-binding and there are no prescribed sanctions for countries that miss them. Countries that lowered their carbon emissions often did so by shifting their polluting industries to other countries. Thus emissions of greenhouse gases continued to rise. Civic recycling programs, while popular and helpful, have not stemmed the tide of waste. In some sense civic recycling programs have served as a distraction: they allow people to believe they are doing their part as individuals, while the problem continues to grow.

Consider, as a specific example, the wildfires which struck the eastern coast of Australia from late 2019 to early 2020. A season of record-high daytime temperatures, regularly above 40 degrees C, and the worst drought in decades, created the perfect conditions for the largest and most destructive bushfires in all of Australia's history, far outstripping the better-publicised wildfires which damaged the Amazon basin, California, and Cameron, earlier in the year. From October of 2019 up to January 2020, every Australian state had large uncontrolled bushfires. By the first days of 2020, more than 5.9 million hectares of bush has been destroyed, entire towns completely destroyed, tens of thousands of people displaced, nineteen people killed, and 28 people were missing. The military was called in to help with evacuations and firefighting work.[189] On New Year's Eve, thousands of evacuees in New South Wales, the area hardest hit, fled to the coast and huddled together overnight on beaches or in small boats, trapped between the fires and the ocean, waiting for larger ships to come and rescue them.[190] An estimated half a billion animals and plants were killed,[191] and over the surrounding oceans the heatwave raised water temperatures enough to kill most marine wildlife.[192] Ash and dust from the fires fell as far away as New Zealand,[193] more than two thousand kilometers away.

Without exaggeration, though it may seem absurd to say it: the wildfires of that season were the most destructive environmental catastrophe in the history of Australia since its colonization by Europeans. But may I draw attention to two more facts about them that are relevant to my argument. The first is that *the wildfires had been predicted twelve years previously,* by the authors of an environmental impact study commissioned by the Australian government.[194] The same researchers provided an update in 2011 which warned: "Even an increase of 2°C above pre-industrial levels would have significant implications for the distribution of rainfall in Australia, the frequency and intensity of flood and drought, the intensity of cyclones and the intensity and frequency of conditions for catastrophic bushfires."[195] The second and more salient fact for my argument is that even while the fires were burning, *Australian Prime Minister Scott Morrison publicly denied the severity of the fires and denied their connection to climate change.* "We have faced these disasters before," he said, waving the fires away as though they were normal and unimportant.[196] Two days later, after receiving some angry heckling from citizens for his comments, he acknowledged the necessity to review "all contributing factors" including climate change. But in the days that followed, he continued to deny direct links between the wildfires and climate change, and repeated his government's support for the fossil fuel industry and his opposition to any emissions-reduction plan.[197] Twenty-four people were charged with arson in relation to the bushfire crisis. But at the same time, an online disinformation campaign exaggerated the role of the arsonists, in order to muddy people's understanding of the relationship between the bushfires and the climate crisis.[198]

The general point: even when a major climate disaster strikes an affluent, well-educated, developed and modern nation populated mostly by White people – the kind of nation one would expect to get the most media attention and to do the most amount of work to protect at least themselves if no one else – still there is no Climate Reckoning. The crisis carries on.

A United Nations report published in 2018 said that humanity must reduce our global carbon output to zero in only twelve years, or else face a future of more droughts, more violent storms, more floods, more refugees and mass migrations, more giant wildfires, more desertification, more ocean acidification, more death, more of everything that is associated with climate change.[199] I have a bold prophesy for you: *we will miss that target.* We will miss it because the people who are in a position to do anything about it are also in a position to insulate themselves and their families from the worst consequences.

Think of it by the following analogy. In the first decade of this century, there were plenty of warning signs that the global financial system was on the verge of breaking. This mostly had to do with sub-prime mortgage lending in the United States, though there were other factors, too. Some of the people who raised the warning were ignored; others were fired or otherwise censured. But the uppermost people knew the warnings were logically sound. They also knew they need not worry, because the government would bail them out. And that is exactly what happened. In the months following the banking crash of 15th September 2008, hundreds of banks and industrial corporations deemed "too big to fail" received bail-out money from the government, sometimes as direct cash injections, sometimes as purchase of shares, so they could continue producing their products and paying their workers and employees. (Many of the executive-level management also pocketed that money for themselves. That's another scandal, but only tangentially relevant to my current argument.)

I think the same thing is going to happen regarding the warnings that the world's climate scientists have sounded since the early 1970's. The super-rich will get a climate change bail-out. Never mind that as a class they are powerful enough to transition the world to a zero-carbon, green energy economy in less than ten years, whilst remaining fabulously rich. Never mind that some of them, taken individually, do care about the health of the planet: Canadian billionaire Chip Wilson bought entire islands in British Columbia in order to protect their endangered ecosystems from logging.[200] *As a class*, they will save themselves first. They will squeeze as much money as they can from the fossil-fuel economy, mostly from the sales of their products but also, significantly, from governments, directly as subsidies or indirectly as tax breaks and taxpayer-funded oil pipelines and other infrastructure. They will use this money to build life-boats for themselves in parts of the world where the effects of the climate crisis are likely to be less intense: New Zealand, for example.[201] In fact, when certain celebrity industrialists say we should colonize Mars to make it harder for some future disaster to destroy the human race,[202] I strongly suspect that the phrase "the human race" does not mean all of us. It means, instead, a select class of uber-wealthy individuals who can pay to jump ship before it catches fire. It would amaze me, but not surprise me, if one or more Mars colonies are already in the early stages of pre-fabrication.

And so we are led to a ninth answer to the root question: *Ecological rage: the anger arising from the knowledge that those in a position to stop the crisis did nothing; the fury that arises from seeing all life on Earth pay for the selfishness and the hubris of the few.*

Elderhood: We Broke The World For Nothing

Let's suppose you're retired now. You've given all your adult years to creating the life you wanted to live, and becoming the person you set out to be. Let's suppose you've been mostly successful. You might have a side-gig to supplement your pension or your savings, but you don't need to work as much. You can stay up late and sleep in late, any day that you like. You can go on longer holidays. You don't have to impress anyone – not that you were ever obliged, but now there is no longer much to be gained by doing so. But your health is not what it once was. Your children have grown and gone. And your future is even more closed now than it was when you were middle aged. So you're writing your last will and testament. You might have twenty more years left to live, but you might equally as likely have only twenty more days. That has always been true, but in your elderhood that fact holds you with greater gravity than ever before.

So you sit back and ask yourself: what was the point?

In the course of building the urban hyper-real and immersing ourselves within it, we broke the planetary circle of life. We have disrupted the functioning of the biosphere to the point where, on the global scale, *it is no longer a circle.* Rather, it has become a through-put of materials, life, and energy, from the biosphere, and into human technologies and consumer markets whose total output is various toxic substances which either directly poison the biosphere, for instance by acidifying soils and waters, or else which disrupts the heat-dissipation pathways of the planet, such as by outputting greenhouse gases or by destroying ecosystems and habitats. Note the word 'total' here is important, since it is easy to find counterexamples on the local scale: wildlife adapted to urban settings, surviving by scavenging our garbage, for instance. But these counter-examples are over-matched by our disruptive effects on higher scales. Indeed, on the global scale, there are no counterexamples.

For another reason: the amount of material and energy that

the urban hyper-real must consume to sustain itself goes far beyond the biosphere's ability to regenerate those materials and energies. In 2021, for example, "Earth Overshoot Day", the day in a given year when humanity's annual consumer demand for the life and matter of the Earth exceeds what the biosphere can regenerate in that same year, fell on the 29th of July.[203] All consumption in 2021 after that date thus counts as earth-destruction and irreplaceable loss – a straight line from life to death, not a circle from life to life. Admittedly, Overshoot Day in 2021 was later (and thus better) than most days in the ten years prior to the Coronavirus pandemic. Nevertheless, if humanity were to temper its consumption-demand to preserve the biosphere's regenerative functions, Overshoot Day would fall upon the 31st of December: or better still, on any day at all in the following year.

For a third: because the functioning of the global biosphere, whose ultimate *telos* is to discharge solar energy as efficiently as possible, has been disrupted past the point where the most efficient pathways to the accomplishment of that *telos* are now destructive to life. Biodiversity loss, desertification, and the frequency and severity of catastrophic tropical storms, are the most important indicators here.

If we were to step outside of the urban hyper-real to grasp the fullness of our being-ecological, to grasp the damage we have wrought upon the circle of life, and to grasp the irretrievability, the permanence, of the loss, *and to grasp that we might have wrought all this damage for nothing,* we should be overcome by ecological grief.

I did not invent the term. Ecological grief is a real emotional and cognitive condition, documented by psychologists, anthropologists, and other researchers, since at least 2017. The most widely accepted academic definition runs as follows: ecological grief is "grief felt in relation to experienced or anticipated ecological losses, including the loss of species, ecosystems and meaningful landscapes due to acute or chronic environmental change."[204] Researchers have recorded it arising in response to a wide variety of events: sea ice loss in the Arctic, drought in Australia's wheat belt, forest fires in northern Canada, the decline of urban wildlife in the United Kingdom, the extinction or extirpation of plants with deep cultural significance to Aboriginal people.[205] Further: a wide variety of people report feeling it: from Indigenous people in Canada, Australia, and elsewhere, whose keen and long-developed perceptual intelligence alerts them to subtle changes in their worlds, to university-based researchers in ecology and climate science with access to statistical databases and satellite imagery, and to the middle-class general public.[206]

I, myself, have it. From 2015 to 2018, I was a regular visitor to a village in central Bohemia, Czech Republic, where I holidayed for the summer, and wrote the bulk of several books. Over those visits I grew to love the landscape. I loved how *explorable* it was. The village is nestled in a shallow valley of meadows and forested hills, and near to a steeper valley which beds the Vltava River. It's as near to a kingdom of magic as I have known since I had to leave the Elora Gorge. It's better than my childhood forest, perhaps, in that it's that much larger, and it's not a simulacra fairyland managed by the tourism industry: it's a real place, and home to modern people. They have solar panels on the roofs. And internet access. But what I loved most was walking the trails and hill crests and cave-like hollow hedgerows, with Helli the wolfdog keeping me company, watching out for whatever may lie ahead. But in 2018, Europe was under a protracted heat wave, and had been since Easter. Daytime temperatures never went below 33°C the whole time I was there; and it rained only once that summer. The grass in the meadows browned and crackled underfoot. The trees withered too, as if autumn was upon us. A local friend told me the price of hay for animal-feed was 20% higher in that year because of drought-induced scarcity. I have known for years that climate change and global warming really is happening. Nevertheless, to see it come to this land that over several years I had grown to love – heartbreaking.

I see another dimension to ecological grief: one which is not documented in academic literature under that name. It reveals itself in questions of an existential nature: *what was all that ecological destruction finally for?* We broke the circle of life by building an urban hyper-reality where affluent people in the developed world could struggle out from their being-ecological and toward their being-free. But did all that wealth-gathering and competition and exploitation make us any happier? Did the creation of the urban hyper-real ease our burdens? Did it help us escape the terror of time and the fear of death? Did it bring us any closer to the gods? Did it provide any clarity on the meaning of life?

No, it didn't.

Perhaps that is one reason many people do not wish to face the climate crisis. Perhaps that is one reason why many people refuse to call it a *crisis* at all. They would rather feel outraged about gas prices, or victimized by "woke" activists, or bored with the banality of pop culture, or frankly to feel anything at all, than to feel despair.

We have seen in a previous meditation how the urban hyper-real could be framed as a triumph of the human spirit. And if nothing else, the urban hyper-reality is exciting. There's always something happening, always something new. It's easy to find people who share your interests and your values; easy to find collaborators for anything you may want to do.

But if the urban hyper-real lifts us out of being-ecological, what are we delivered *into*? Our being-free. But what is the world of the human being-free? As we have seen, it is a world of Platonic geometry and techno-digital theatre. Such a world can be, and often is, oppressive, constraining, even *inhuman*. It might exclude expressions of spontaneous organic messiness, and interfere with our ability to carry on an original relationship with reality. The Viennese architect and painter Friedensreich Hundertwasser condemned the "jungle of straight lines, which increasingly hems us in like prisoners in a gaol...The straight line is not a creative, but a reproductive line. In it dwells not so much God and the human spirit as rather the comfort-loving, brainless mass ant."[207] Karsten Harries acknowledged that view: "the problem with this Platonism is that, while it perhaps answers to the demands of the spirit, it short-changes the whole human being. We are after all not angels, and we don't need ethereal homes fit only for angels."[208] But I think the strongest reply comes from a philosopher who, in other respects, regarded techno-rationality as a fundamental feature of human nature: Martin Heidegger.

We've seen him in these meditations before, and I haven't been friendly to his ideas. Yet there is one place where, I feel awkward to admit, he was exactly correct: *modern technology stockpiles human beings as raw materials.* The urban hyper-real treats human beings as raw materials, no less than no less than the resources of the Earth. Not that this didn't happen in pre-modern societies: slavery, corvée labour, forced marriage, and other forms of human stockpiling is as old as civilization itself. But Heidegger shows what is distinctive about its modern version. "The essence of modern technology," he says, "starts man upon the way of that revealing through which the actual everywhere, more or less distinctly, becomes standing reserve".[209] We have seen how, in a disenchanted world, the value of everything is in its utility and possessability, and nothing else. Here we must go further: in the "free" world of the urban hyper-real, human beings, no less than a stockpile of natural resources, will be valued according to their utility and possessability, and nothing else. Heidegger says:

As soon as what is unconcealed [ie. harvested raw materials from the Earth] no longer concerns man even as object, but does so, rather, exclusively as standing-reserve, and man in the midst of objectlessness is nothing but the orderer of the standing-reserve, then he comes to the very brink of it precipitous fall; that is, *he comes to the point where he himself will have to be taken as standing-reserve* ... Where this ordering holds sway, it drives out every other possibility of revealing.[210]

The urban hyper-real stockpiles human beings in exactly the way Heidegger describes. In its grip we are always selected, numbered, processed, labelled, categorized, and classified: and this process of human stockpiling displaces the more human relationships of understanding, considering, caring, and knowing. In Heidegger's time the dominant human-stockpiling forces were the army, the industrial assembly line, and, lest we forget, the concentration camps (not only in Nazi-occupied Europe, but also the gulags in Russia, and the internment camps for Japanese immigrants in Canada and the United States). Today the dominant forces are the security state, social media, and the precariat service-economy job. In the security state, everyone is presumed to be a potential terrorist, if not an actual one. This is especially visible in airports, where people are identified, screened, assessed, X-rayed, monitored, ticketed, herded, classified, and segregated, before they are deemed trustworthy enough to be packaged for delivery. Even for the first-class passengers, this is a disciplinary technique: its effect is to train people to comply with authority. In social media, each user's qualities, preferences, and values – even her very identity – is mathematically quantified from thousands of data-points extracted from photos, comments, interactions, keywords, friend-connections, followings, and GPS-tracked movements through space. Her time and attention is held by the deliberately-addictive properties of the medium, and sold to advertisers like any other consumer product sold by a retailer to a customer. In the geometric-mechanical space of the city, the dominant stockpiling force is the precariat service-industry job. This force is most visible when the workers are treated as "free" independent contractors instead of as employees, so that labour rights like minimum wage, safety training, scheduled breaks, and so on, don't apply. It also appears when workers are given zero-hour contracts, or compelled to wear digital tracking devices to monitor productivity, or required to use their own social media pages to advertise the employer's products. Most of all, it appears when the cost of food and housing is so high that fully-employed workers must nonetheless draw upon public welfare to survive.

We broke the biosphere of our planet in order to create a world of stockpiled human beings in precarious wage-slave jobs for the benefit of a small class of uber-wealthy men, whose designs for the future involve fixing the stockpiling as a permanent feature of reality, glamorizing it, and elevating themselves to godhood. "Meanwhile man, precisely as the one so threatened, exalts himself to the posture of lord of the earth."[211]

Thus we come to the tenth answer to my root question. What human reality emerges from the encounter with the Earth? *Ecological grief; the despair of witnessing the broken-ness of the Earth; the despair of realizing that we might have broken the Earth for nothing.*

One Question, Many Answers

Who faces the Earth? What becomes of the human reality when facing the Earth? A simple question, but it produced a long list of complicated answers.

In the meditation on birth, we discovered the human reality becomes a situation of tragic giftedness.

In infancy, we discovered a new form of being-ecological, which I called perceptual intelligence.

In childhood, we found that human society undergoes an ecological succession of culture, measured by and driven by language. We also discovered prospects for magic and play, awaiting beyond the boundaries of the human world.

In adolescence, the human world swallowed everything, leaving us disenchanted, dwelling in a space defined by mere objects and impersonal facts.

Reaching adulthood, we discovered how work can make us masters of the world, and this gave us a sense of confidence and entitlement. Our being-ecological was, by this point, so far out of sight, that we lost our knowledge of what the World of Earth is really like.

In our middle age, we saw what became of that work, and of that ignorance. We created for ourselves a fully humanized world, an urban hyper-reality, and we found ourselves trapped in it. Looking outside that reality, we find the full scale of the climate crisis, and the full scale of the injustice behind it, and so we felt enraged.

In our old age, we realised that the urban hyper-reality did not help us lead better lives; we realised we may have broken the Circle of Life for nothing. This realization, combined with the realization of what we have lost of the World of Earth, led us to despair.

One question, ten answers. As you can see, they followed a progression, from a close overlap between our being-ecological and our being-free, to ever further distances between them. Yet they have something in common: each of them is a response to the Earth; a response to the state of things around us. Each is also indicative and constitutive of who we are as human beings, at different times in our lives or under different circumstances.

From here, I think we need to search for a new human reality: one which faces and responds to the climate crisis; one which perceives the broken-ness of the Circle of Life as a kind of call for help; one which closes the distance between our being-ecological and our being-free without retreating into illusion, rage, or despair. So that life everywhere, including human life, can reach for and achieve its potential for *eudaimonia*, the flourishing and worthwhile life.

That new human reality is likely to be as multi-coloured, diverse, and unpredictable, as any ecosystem recovering from a disturbance, even with the pursuit of *eudaimonia* as the engine of its *aletheia*. I should not presume to predict its exact contours. But think that I can trace a path to reach it. The tracing of the path shall be the task of my third root question. So here we go!

Third Root Question

Can The Circle Be Healed?

Reality never unfolds itself only one petal at a time. Reality unfolds in meadows, forests of wildflowers, butterflies, chipmunks, trees, and weeds, all in their many colours and relations. New leaves turn over in the distance before they can be studied up close; a wolf is heard howling in the distance before he is seen. Thus during the COVID-19 pandemic, while most of us grasped reality through the limiting frames of our apartment windows and computer screens, reality revealed new faces to us. With most of the developed world's population staying home, humanity's total consumption of the Earth fell by 9.3%.[212] Roads and highways emptied of car traffic, and the skies emptied of aircraft. Traffic in Montreal, for example, dropped to 56% of its normal rush hour congestion.[213] International passenger flights fell by 40%.[214] As a result, smog levels fell, and visibility improved. In Punjab, India, for example, residents of most towns in Doaba region could see the entire Dhauladhar range of the Himalayan mountains, more than 100km away: a sight normally possible only when local smog had been cleared by rainfall (and even then, only a few peaks are visible, not the entire length and height).[215] In Delhi, where the air quality index on a good day is around 200 (and anything above 25 is considered unsafe), the index fell to 20: skies were blue again, and stars were visible at night.[216] Los Angeles, California, one of the most smog-polluted cities in the world, became one of the clearest: overall air quality improved 20%, and PM 2.5 pollution dropped 40%. The city enjoyed its longest uninterrupted stretch of "good" air since 1995.[217] Then there were the changes in government policy. Financial assistance packages, such as the Canada Emergency Response Benefit, enabled people thrown out of work by the quarantine to buy food and pay rent. Banks gave landlords temporary relief from mortgage payments. Student loan repayments were suspended.

Newly revealed realities like these, and our responses to them, made previously unthinkable and impossible social changes thinkable and possible.

These new realities inspired people to imagine, for example, that government programs like the Canada Emergency Response Benefit could be extended indefinitely, or even transformed into something like a universal basic income.[218] To choose another example: as global emissions of CO_2 fell during the pandemic by 17%,[219] people realised that the other 83% was not coming from their cars. By March of 2021, global CO_2 concentrations had reached yet another record high: 417.14 parts per million,[220] even though the pandemic was into its third wave. So if all that greenhouse gas was not coming from people's cars, where was it coming from? The only other remaining sources are electric power generation, agriculture, and manufacturing. The old argument that pollution and global warming is caused by mass consumerism, was shown to be much weaker than previously believed. Industry had more responsibility than anyone in mainstream politics had previously acknowledged. There were widespread calls to speed up the process of transitioning the global energy industry away from fossil fuels and toward renewables like wind and solar. Interest increased for new forms of nuclear power, such as the travelling-wave reactor and various passive-nuclear systems, which cannot melt down, and which do not require the complex back-up systems of reactors designed in the 1950s.[221]

New realities prompted new thoughts and new possibilities. Unthinkable actions became thinkable.

To be sure, many, probably most people, had too much new stress in their lives to do any abstract social-political speculating. But I think it is worth observing that *we now live in an age where nothing in politics is unthinkable.* Today, even the wildest propositions are on the table. Including, as we saw in 2020, the disbanding or drastic reduction of militarized police forces, in the wake of the murder of George Floyd on 25th May of that year. Also including, as we saw in 2017, cages and concentration camps to imprison migrant children.

Nothing is unthinkable anymore. So I encourage everyone reading these words to think big.

The philosopher Hegel coined the memorable proverb: "The owl of Minerva takes its flight only when the shades of night are gathering." Though this phrase has had many meanings over time, I believe it says: when things are bad, new ideas and new possibilities emerge. Well, my friends, night has fallen. It's time to get to work. For a philosopher, 'getting to work' means thinking big.

So in these last few meditations I will offer *proposals* as well as arguments. Some of them will be based on things that are already happening; some will be my ideas. You might find that some of mine are more than a little wild and crazy. But I hope that you find them big. As a guiding principle to judge them: consider whether there are less radical proposals which can heal the Circle of Life more completely and in less time.

So. In addition to all the usual things environmental activists recommend, I hereby propose:

- Governments should establish an organized body of scientists, researchers, scouts, signaleers, educators, engineers, park rangers, investigators, enforcement officers, and workers, to act as the nation's primary environmental protection force. Let's call this body "The Earth Keepers". Its mission: to monitor environmental quality and attain total situational awareness of all significant ecological disturbances in the nation's territory; to restore and rewild all poisoned or abandoned lands; to advocate on behalf of landscapes, waters, wildlife, and ecosystems; to install ecology-based defences against the climate crisis; to provide assistance and defence to communities suffering environmental emergencies; to gather intelligence on polluters and other environmental offenders for use by criminal prosecutors; and to interdict environmental offenders. Some of these functions are already performed by other agencies, such as the police. Some Indigenous communities have Land Defenders who perform similar functions, often to the inconvenience of oil companies and logging companies. The idea of gathering these functions into a single service is to grant these functions more prestige and visibility, and more resources: the Earth Keepers should be the kind of institution that can claim to represent the best of a nation's energies, technologies, talent, and character, on par with its army and its public health-care service. I'm comparing the Earth Keepers to the army for a reason. The ability to fight, to survive a battlefield, and to kill, should not be the only things that a society valorizes. Protecting the Earth from environmental offenders and from the climate crisis is 'defending the country' too.

- The United Nations should create global ecological commons, to include one-half of all international waters, and one-third of the land surface of the earth, that is *absolutely off-limits to all forms of heavy industry and urbanization.* The purpose of the commons is to give the earth space to regenerate itself and bear humanity's weight. The only economic activities allowable should be small-scale farming, subsistence hunting and fishing, low-impact tourism, and traditional practices carried on by Aboriginal people. Areas selected for this absolute protection should be distributed across the Earth: they should be areas of greatest biodiversity, greatest contribution to climate system regulation, significant scientific interest, and significant cultural meaning for Indigenous people. These areas should be monitored and patrolled by orbital satellites, the armed forces, Indigenous land defenders, and/or the Earth Keepers, to prevent poaching, illegal industries, illegal waste dumping, and the like.

- Dismantle the fossil fuel energy industry and replace it with wind, wave, solar, and geothermal energy, and with the current generation of nuclear power. Energy production can then be increased in order to help eliminate poverty without at the same time contributing to the climate crisis.[222]

- Phase out all fossil-fuel vehicles, and replace them with electric vehicles.

- Phase out industrial agriculture, and replace it with regenerative agriculture and tree intercropping. These practices have been shown to reduce agricultural carbon outputs, prevent erosion, and prevent soil microbiome damage. Crucially, they are shown to be *capable of feeding every human being alive on Earth today*.[223]

- Clean water for drinking, cleaning, and bathing, should be declared a human right. All communities should have clean water delivery and sewer systems installed (some First Nations communities in Canada do not have these services, even to this day). All corporations that provide water on a for-profit basis should have that part of their business turned over to public management, or else dismantled.

- The commercial water-bottling industry should cease all production. Its infrastructure should be brought under democratic control, and operated as a not-for-profit public service, with its volume of production scaled down so as not to drain aquifers nor to compete with municipal household water services.

- Legal personhood should be granted to landforms and land-features including rivers, lakes, mountains, and critical ecosystems, as already happens in Quebec, New Zealand, Ecuador, Bolivia, and elsewhere in the world.[224] Ecuador includes rights for nature in Article 72 of its 2008 constitution. Legal personhood for landforms allows those landforms (as represented by environmental action groups and their lawyers) to sue for damages.

- A global 'Green New Deal', along the lines proposed in 2019 by US Congresswoman Alexandria Ocasio-Cortez and her associates, should be adopted into law worldwide.

- Billions of trees must be planted all over the world: a re-forestation effort on the scale larger than the Great Green Wall of China and the Great Green Wall of the Sahara. Tree-planting, re-foresting, rewilding, and bio-remediation are the most efficient and the most cost-effective ways to capture and sequester carbon out of the atmosphere and to restore biodiversity. There is no human-made technology at this time which can capture and sequester carbon more efficiently than a tree. (Note, however, that tree-planting is not a substitute for reducing industrial carbon outputs, because trees have limits to how much carbon they can capture. The goal here is to reduce the total carbon volume in the cycle, not simply to increase sequestration capacity. And trees cannot sequester carbon if a heat wave sets them on fire.)

Ecofascism Is Not Environmentalism

Martin Heidegger's work has enjoyed a recent resurgence of interest among ecologists and environmental thinkers. He was among the philosophers cited by the founders of Deep Ecology as inspirational, perhaps because his work can be read as an attempt to overcome the Cartesian dualism of subject-and-object, observer-and-observed, which many Deep Ecologists regard as part of the problem with Western philosophy.[225] Ecology is a science of relationships; its spirit teaches that everyone and everything is a participant in the world, everyone is involved, everyone is enmeshed and entwined together, up close or at a distance, one way or another. Ecology is an intrinsically anti-fascist science.

Some of Heidegger's ideas seem to resonate with that view. His concept of *Dasein* means 'being-in-the-world' *on the Earth*. In his essay *The Origin of the Work of Art*, he says: "Upon the earth and in it, historical man grounds his dwelling in the world... The work [of art] moves the earth itself into the open region of a world and keeps it there. The work lets the earth be an earth.[226] Similarly Heidegger says that in *Dasein* there is no question of higher or lower beings, or any hierarchy in the essence of being.[227] We could, perhaps, use that premise to generate a kind of authenticity, an original relationship with Being, if only we ceased interfering with things and let them reveal themselves according to their own ways of being in the world. *But that kind of authenticity is not Heidegger's ultimate aim.* As we have seen, Heidegger regarded the absorption of all the resources of the Earth into standing-reserves, and the absorption of human beings too, as inevitable. There is, in his philosophy, no escape from technology. And while he regarded that inevitability as bad, still he resolves the horror of his own conclusion by suggesting that the things-of-earth, and other people too, somehow *grant* themselves, or give permission, to be absorbed:

> Every destining of revealing [ie, every inevitable *aletheia*] comes to pass from out of a granting and as such a granting. For it is granting that first conveys to man that share in revealing which the coming-to-pass of revealing needs. As the one so needed and used, man is given to belong to the

coming-to-pass of truth [*aletheia*]. The granting that sends us in one way or another into revealing is as such the saving power. For the saving power lets man see and enter into the highest dignity of his essence.[228]

Heidegger's hypnotic prose expresses the dark idea that the things-of-earth, and indeed human beings, invite us, or even want us, to capture and possess them. *The earth wants no such thing. Nor do any oppressed people.* It is we, imagining ourselves as lords of the earth, who want to capture and possess things. It is we who invent the invitation from God or from our victims to validate the possession. The most that we can claim here with any logical consistency is that under the aspect of work, the things-of-earth appear available, useful, malleable, and possessable. But we cannot say that the things-of-earth are granted to us. Under the aspect of work, things have no spirit of their own, no magic, no independent *aletheia*. The only consistent way to say that something is 'granted' in that sense is to say that no one else has yet laid a claim upon it. But that is a response to the moral call of people and society, not to the moral call of the Earth itself. If the Earth, as an Immensity, wants anything, it wants to enact the Twelve Ways to Ecology: to reveal itself, to cooperate and to compete, to pass on what it gathers, and to carry on. In terms of its relation to us, it wants to engage with us as a symbiotic partner; it wants to be understood, protected, cared for, and loved.

However, as observed earlier, Heidegger also said that it's *modern* technology which brings the danger. There is another kind of technology, *techne* as *poesis*, 'poetry', which he says can allow people to enter a more authentic relationship with the earth. Ecologists and philosophers often cite this angle in his work for inspiration. What they miss is that for Heidegger only one kind of society can give you *techne* as *poesis*: national socialism.[229] "From a metaphysical point of view," he wrote in

Introduction to Metaphysics, "Russia [communist totalitarianism] and America [capitalism and democracy] are the same; the same dreary technological frenzy, the same unrestricted organization of the average man". And in a lecture he gave in 1943: "The planet is in flames, the essence of man is out of joint. World-historical thinking can come only from the Germans – if, that is, they find and preserve 'the German essence' (*das Deutsche*)."[230] As late as 1966, in an interview with *Der Spiegel* which, by his request, was not published until after his death, Heidegger said: "I see the situation of man in the world of planetary technicity not as an inextricable and inescapable destiny, but I see the task of thought precisely in this, that within its own limits it helps man as such achieve a satisfactory relationship to the essence of technicity. National Socialism did indeed go in this direction."[231]

Heidegger did immediately clarify that "those people [the Nazis], however, were far too poorly equipped for thought..." Still, ecologists and philosophers who look to Heidegger for inspiration are looking into an abyss. Heidegger's questions concerning the Earth were not only about reclaiming a lost original relationship with Being. They were also about painting intellectual glamour upon ethnic nationalism (*Volksgemeinschaft*), precisely in accord with the platform of the NSDAP. The publication in 2014 of his diaries, the 'Black Notebooks', makes that clear: in those diaries he re-affirmed his anti-Semitism, and excluded the Jews from the possibility of possessing an authentic relationship with Being.[232]

I might have ignored this theme in Heidegger's work, and indeed ignored Heidegger completely, if it were not the case that in environmental debates today, the ugly head of fascism has returned. And this resurgent fascism is reading Heidegger, too; it's borrowing his prestige as a top-rank philosopher in order to appear intellectual and rational. In some sense, ecofascism has been with us for a very long time. Many early American conservationists, including Gifford Pinchot and Madison Grant, were also committed eugenicists; Grant published a book on white supremacy called *The Passing Of The Great Race* (1916).[233] In 1968 the biologist Paul Ehrlich published *The Population Bomb*, a work of unashamed xenophobia which distracted much of the environmental debate for the next half-century. Its thesis is that all public problems, not only environmental degradation but also war, poverty, political conflict, *everything*, was caused by poor people in poor countries having too many children, and that a complete social collapse was therefore immanent. Garret Hardin, creator of the famous Tragedy of the Commons, continued the argument in his 1974 essay *Lifeboat Ethics: The Case Against Helping The Poor*. He argued that people in poor nations reproduce too fast, and therefore ought to be left to starve and die in order to prevent ecological catastrophe.[234] And as a final example: the terrorist who murdered forty-nine Muslims in Christchurch, New Zealand, in 2019, freely described himself as an ecofascist. He published a manifesto, *The Great Replacement*, in which he wrote: "There is no Green future with never ending population growth... Continued immigration into Europe is environmental warfare and ultimately destructive to nature itself." He therefore advised his readers to "Kill the invaders, kill the overpopulation and by doing so save the environment".[235]

'Population', and 'overpopulation', does not explain human impacts on the biosphere. The ecofascists repeat this meme as if a single word could explain a multi-tentacled hyperobject like the climate crisis. The true nature of the problem can be revealed by examining the *nature of the demand* human beings impose on the biosphere. The first fact is that human demands on the environment *are not evenly distributed across all groups, classes, and nations.* The people whom the ecofascists want to see dead are people who, because of their poverty, contribute almost nothing to the climate crisis, both individually and as a group. The second fact is that the wealthiest 10% of humanity are so rich their impact on the climate crisis is greater than the other 90% combined.

Thus the problem is not 'overpopulation': it is income inequality and excessive wealth stratification. This has been extensively studied by economists, social scientists, and mathematicians; there is no significant doubt about it in academic circles.[236] Rage against 'overpopulation' is not environmentalism. It is racism dressed up in green clothing, and nothing else.

The problem is not, as Heidegger supposed, that we have somehow lost our original relationship with Being. The problem is not overpopulation, and not multiculturalism, as supposed by the ecofascists. *The problem is that the circle of life is broken.* Hatred cannot save the Earth, for hatred cannot heal. In fact, hatred cannot deliver a good life to the ecofascists themselves. It is, in the original Pagan sense, a vice; a quality that punishes its possessors by excluding them from their own eudaimonia. All it can do is stoke obsessions, amplify fears, impress the gullible, incentivize foolishness, divide communities, and glamorize violence. In sum, all it can do is destroy.

So here is a first answer to the third root question: Can we heal the Circle of Life? – *Yes, if we reject ecofascism, reduce income inequality, and reject any worldview that endorses hatred in even the smallest way.*

To that end, I propose:

- The enactment of laws which require that elected politicians receive salaries of no greater than ten times the minimum wage, and that the directors of corporations receive salaries no greater than ten times the lowest-paid employee of that corporation. (So if you're rich and you want to get richer, you have to pay your people more.)
- The closure of all tax loopholes for the wealthy, including offshore tax havens and shell corporations.
- There are laws that allow corporations to sue governments for 'loss of future profits' when governments close or

regulate a high-polluting industry. All these laws must be repealed. Cases before the courts which are based on these laws must be dismissed.

- The creation of a global ecological commons royalty, such that a fraction of all the profit from the exploitation of resources taken from the Earth, and from moons and asteroids and other bodies in space, shall be given to ecological restoration projects, and also paid as a basic income to every human being on earth.

- The creation of a global cultural institution which encourages, celebrates, rewards, and shares works of artistic excellence that arise from healthy interpersonal, social, cultural, and human-ecological relations, and which has more funding and more communications-reach (more "market share") than that which is available to the publishers of disinformation, fake news, and anti-green propaganda.

- The regulation of social media to prevent fake news, disinformation, and lies, in the same manner as broadcast and print media is regulated. The freedom of expression, and of the press, should be preserved, of course; but it should be guided back to its original purpose, which is to improve the quality of individual and public rationality, and to allow the best ideas to rise to prominence regardless of their compatibility with state policies or corporate interests.

The Gatekeepers of Human Nature

"Deep ecology", though the name is a misnomer, at least has this in its favour: it asks people to go back to first principles, to the deep roots of their world views, for answers to philosophical questions about climate ethics. But I think it reaches a dead end in its proposal that we could evolve out of parasitism and into symbiosis if only we changed our world views. As if such a thing is easy to do! Strong historical, cultural, religious, and economic forces push people to preserve and to further reinforce the very world views that Deep Ecology identifies as part of the problem. One might as well call for the creation of a brand-new religion, a brand-new political culture, a brand-new narrative of the human condition. Many philosophers, activists, artists, and the like, have called for that new narrative. Plenty of small communities on the fringes of the mainstream have experimented with them, with varying degrees of small-scale success. But so far, no new narrative has proven strong enough to dislodge the uber-narrative of consumer capitalism.

Instead of agitating to change everyone's worldview in the hope that governments, corporations, markets, and other institutions will follow on their own, I propose we change the public conditions in which worldviews arise in the first place. This means, among other things, understanding what those public conditions are, and how they influence people's worldviews. I shall begin the analysis with the following axiom: that there is no such thing as human nature, writ large upon our species as a whole. This I take to be self-evident: for any given claim about human nature, there is an equal and opposite empirical observation. Individual natures exist: individual people have their own unique footsteps, gestures, tones of voice, attitudes, habits, and the like, by which you can tell who someone is, and by which you can make some broad predictions about how they will behave. And, instinctual habits exist: this is how you can cross a crowded road without bumping into things and without really looking. But 'human nature', as an *universal* set of wants and behaviours and emotional dispositions, does not exist. For every argument that we human beings are altruistic and kind, there is evidence of human cruelty. For every argument that we are naturally self-centred and materialistic, there is evidence of generosity and love.

And yet so much of our economics, politics, religions, and

worldviews, make strong claims about human nature as a whole, and with at least *some* empirical evidence in support. Where, then, do these claims come from? I think it comes from a process like the following.

1. Although we do not have a general, species-wide nature, we do have general, species-wide *needs*: to eat, to sleep, to shelter from danger, to remove waste, and so on. We also need companionship, respect, knowledge, and meaning. Let us call something a need if deprivation of that thing leads to the loss of capacity to think, to feel, and/or to move through space, up to and including the loss of life itself.[237] This leads me to the next proposition.

2. In every generation, people are born with every kind of nature. Some are selfish, greedy, or miserly; some are generous, compassionate, and empathetic; some are adventurous, excitable, and energetic; some are melancholic, introverted, and contemplative; and so on. Every generation produces some number of people who will grow into each of these individual natures, and into other natures that may exist beside these.

3. For every type of individual human nature, there also exists a corresponding *want*. For example, the curious nature wants knowledge, the affectionate nature wants love, the spirited nature wants excitement, and so on. Some wants will also be needs, but the overlap is only partial. You need nutritious food, but you want filet mignon; you need meaning in your life, but you want validation. You may also want things that have nothing to do with your needs. You may want, for instance, to win a running race, but your need for health and well-being, or your need for friendship and respect, might not be fulfilled by winning, unless there are some other outstanding circumstances involved. And you could

fulfill your need for friendship and respect in other ways.

4. In every environment into which we are thrown, there are boundaries, barriers, choke-points, and distances, standing between us and the places where both wants and needs may be fulfilled. Let us call these places 'gates'. For example, the geographic distance between your dwelling-place, and the landscapes where your food comes from, is a gate. Farmer's markets, grocery stores, distribution depots, health inspectors, processing plants, and whole systems of food supply management, contain multiple gates. Your food has to pass muster at every gate in order to reach you. Or, if not the food, then you yourself must pass muster, in order to fulfill your wants and needs. You must have enough money to buy what you want; you must ignore other shoppers; you must tolerate the muzak enforcing an artificial happy feeling on your mind. Some retailers might require that you dress properly: no shirt, no shoes, no service!

5. Those people whose individual natures are ambitious, or opportunistic, domineering, attention-seeking, wealth-seeking, greedy, even sociopathic, or some combination of these and similar natures, find that they can fulfill the wants associated with those natures by standing guard on one or more of those aforementioned gates. Let us call these people 'gatekeepers'. These gatekeepers become, in effect, additional gates which people and materials and energy must cross. As such, these gatekeepers possess *power*. Like toll booth operators or ticket collectors, the gatekeepers demand things from all who would pass through their station: for example, money, political or religious obedience, the adoption of a tribal identity, some mode of behaviour.

Politicians are the obvious examples of gatekeepers here. But the gatekeepers can come in many forms and exist on all scales of society, from families and local communities, to international alliances. They can be shopkeepers, business operators, school teachers, college professors, landlords, bosses, priests and clergy, parents, schoolyard bullies, and so on. They can also be corporate executives, broadcasters, military commanders, celebrities, and icons. What matters is how visible they are, and how they stand between you and the fulfillment of your needs for food, shelter, clothing, other material goods, as well as your needs for information, community belonging, and meaning.

6. The gatekeepers, insofar as they are successful over time, conflate their wants and their needs, and conflate their own individual natures with an imagined universal nature for all humanity. They deceive others as well as themselves into believing there is no difference between their wants and their needs. They deceive everyone into thinking that everyone's nature is the same as their own. Thus if it happens that their natures are domineering, self-centered, sociopathic, or otherwise vicious, they will incentivise others around them to become similarly vicious. If their natures are rational, generous, humane, empathetic, or otherwise virtuous, they incentivise virtue.

7. The particular model of human nature embodied by the most successful gatekeepers comes to be adopted by others. This adoption comes about through the requirements and demands the gatekeepers impose on others, as well as the habits people form by fulfilling them. It also comes about through the example and the precedent the gatekeepers set, and the extent to which they can demonstrate to others that their individual natures have led to success in the pursuit of their wants and needs.

8. The power of the successful gatekeepers compounds over time, as it propagates through several generations and acquires the momentum of history and tradition. But due to the shifting of the baseline, no one notices this compounding of attitudes.

9. Thus the individual natures of the gatekeepers come to be seen as the nature of all humanity. Whether or not by deliberate intention on the gatekeeper's part, the community comes to believe that human nature writ-large is whatever the gatekeepers say it is. The gatekeepers themselves come to appear as embodiments of universal humanity, embodiments of the fundamental nature within everyone, embodiments of the fully civilized person.

10. All statements purporting to describe the universal human nature are, in fact, claims describing a particular individual type of human nature which happened to lead to success *for the gatekeepers*, in a particular social and cultural environment, and at a particular time in history. If we human beings are in general rational, enlightened, moral, selfish, competitive, indifferent, compassionate, imaginative, foolish, or of any other general character, it is because we have made ourselves so, through our dealings with the gates, their changing shape over time, and the influence of the gatekeepers who stand upon them.

This, I think, suggests another answer to the third root question of these meditations. Can we heal the Circle of Life? *Yes – if we install the kinds of gatekeepers in our society who encourage, reward, and support environmental healing.* Change the gatekeepers, or change the nature of their influence upon society and culture, and you can change people's habits too.

To that end, I propose:

- Ecological knowledge, including Indigenous ecological knowledge, should be integrated into all levels of primary and secondary education. Every school child should visit an ecologically conserved area for several days of outdoor education at least once a year, in every year of their primary education. Private and elite-private schools shall be granted no exceptions.

- All corporations should be transformed into public-benefit corporations, such that shareholders do not get dividends and executives do not get bonuses unless relevant social and environmental indicators meet or exceed certain scientifically-established and democratically-regulated thresholds.

- Corporations who contribute to the climate crisis should be banned from participating in climate policy discussions at all levels of government, and from all international climate policy conferences. This follows the lead of Glasgow City Council, who in 2021 banned such corporations from public venues during the COP26 world environmental conference.[238]

- Politicians who deny the reality of the climate crisis should be voted out of office. Similarly, politicians who imagine that the crisis will fix itself, whether by natural processes, market forces, future technological innovation, the hand of God, or some other kind of fantasy thinking, should be voted out.

- Corporate executives whose companies are found guilty of environmental damage should go to jail.

- Ecocide, as a category of criminal offence, should be integrated into all national laws, and prosecuted. The model to follow here is the International Criminal Court in The Hague, which in June of 2021 proposed the following definition of ecocide: "unlawful or wanton acts committed with knowledge that there is a substantial likelihood of severe and widespread or long-term damage to the environment being caused by those acts."[239]

- Religious believers should walk away from any religious clergyperson who teaches them to ignore the climate crisis and await salvation in the next life. Believers should simply get up and leave, even in the middle of a service. Believers can re-congregate later, after having replaced the clergy-person, or after finding a new place of assembly elsewhere.

- Education should be made more accessible for women and girls, especially in poor countries. This may seem irrelevant to the climate crisis. However, this has been shown to benefit local ecosystems as well as communities, more so than providing the same benefits to boys. Educated girls are less likely to marry while still children, and less likely to marry against their will; hence they have fewer children. Furthermore, their agricultural plots produce more food and less waste.[240]

Face the Immensity

Banishing the eco-fascists and promoting better people as gatekeepers are only first steps. The substantial work of healing the Circle of Life comes from reducing the tension between our being-ecological and our being-free. It comes from doing things which help fit humanity, individually and together, into a more symbiotic relationship with the earth, while at the same time fulfilling the human needs that arise from our being-free. And it comes from things which deliver more meaning in life, to more people, more of the time, than can be delivered by the destructive identity politics of eco-fascism, the alluring glamour of the urban hyper-real, and the naked greed of consumer capitalism.

So, nothing simple, alas.

One way to do that might be to lean harder into a pure anthropocentric view. We could say: Our lives as human beings depend on the Circle of Life. Therefore we should heal the Circle as a matter of pure self-interest; a matter of benefitting ourselves. This strategy could succeed if *and only if* we are also able to overcome the illusion of infinite carrying capacity. If too many people remain committed to that illusion, and especially if too many people in positions of power and influence (that is, the gatekeepers) remain committed to it, then this strategy will fail.

Another way might be to lean harder into some form of ecocentrism. We could say: the world is beautiful, wondrous, surprising, awe-inspiring, intrinsically valuable, a source of spiritual fulfillment, possibly a home to the gods and many other spiritual beings – in a word, *enchanted*. These qualities have great moral significance: they grant their possessors the right to protection, care, and respect. If we restored in our culture the sense that the Earth is enchanted, we might be more careful and respectful about the feelings and needs of our non-human relatives on the tree of life, and the landscapes in which they dwell. Being more respectful, we might be less exploitative of the Earth, and less casual about the damage we cause.

Although I think this idea is beautiful and could be effective, there are several significant criticisms that deserve attention. Foremost among them: (1), this idea will fail to persuade people who are not already predisposed to it. No amount of insisting that the world is enchanted will convince anyone who cannot, or will not, see it that way. (2), Re-enchantment could help us want to heal the Circle of Life. But as already noted, the political usefulness of an idea should not be the sole foundation of its rationality. (3), If we re-enchant the world by simply *declaring* that the world is enchanted, instead of by *discovering* whether it is so, then the magic will arise from us, our being-free, and not from the world, and not from our being-ecological. If we pretend otherwise, we will commit what philosopher Jean-Paul Sartre calls *bad faith:* a kind of cognitive dissonance or false consciousness that arises from self-deception. (4), Some of the work needed to heal the Circle of Life is work that only large organizations like governments and corporations can do. If we emphasize re-enchantment, we will move responsibility away from those large organizations, and back in the hands of local individuals, who may not be influential or knowledgeable enough to do the job. Re-enchantment might move you to protect a particular tree, a city park, a local wetland. *But we need to protect the entire planet.* (5), Enchantment is like a genie in a bottle: your wish might be granted in ways that you don't expect and which could cause you more trouble in the long run. For example, a strong religious belief that the Circle of Life is under threat might lead to misanthropy and violence. The idea of an enchanted world would have to be presented carefully, with clear principles and mature influencers in its community, to help prevent it from devolving into ecofascism. (6), It is possible for enchantment itself to be captured, co-opted, commodified, and stockpiled, no less than lumber or fish or human beings. We might go looking for a magic forest, and find instead The Magic Forest Experience, a theme park or a computer-generated simulation. There would be ticket gates, purchase prices, designer trees, trained animals, tour guides in costume, a soundtrack issuing from hidden speakers, and an exit through the gift shop. Being enclosed within the hyper-real, people might grow to love the theme-park version of nature more than the original nature. And (7), It would take a long time to change our culture such that more people felt the magic of the Earth, and thus felt the moral call to protect it. *We do not have enough time.* Tipping points are about to be crossed, or have already been crossed. Cultural change must be part of the long-term solution, but other efforts must have priority in the short term.

So, re-enchanting the world won't move us enough to do enough about the climate crisis.

And yet – and yet – there remains an unconquerable sacredness about the Earth, and about its life. As we have seen, there is a special kind of magic that appears in forests, meadows, starry nights, and the like, which does not appear in cities, nor in any part of the human world. It's subtle, fragile, easy to miss. Even a whispered word can shatter it. And yet it persists. So what is it?

In order to satisfy the counterarguments noted above, this deeper kind of enchantment has to be the kind of event which: (1) isn't a matter of relativist or subjective opinion; (2) doesn't reduce to instrumentality, since that is part of what broke the Circle; (3) can move people to care about the earth and to protect it; (4) speaks to the needs of our being-ecological *and* our being-free; and which (5) everyone, including the disenchanted, can experience.

To my mind, that deeper kind of enchantment arises from the Earth itself, the planet as a whole, from its wonderful wild spaces that begin at the edge of the human world and which carry on past the horizon of the seen and the unseen, to the whole biosphere and to the cosmos beyond. The Earth is always greater than any single person's ability to grasp in its totality in a single lifetime. Even for astronauts who can witness the totality from orbit, there is always more to see, more to discover, more to know. It exists on a time scale of billions of years: an effective immortality, from the human point of view. Its complex systems and emergent properties work together as if it is a single living organism: hence any of its creatures or weather-events can hint at the possibility of more going on around the corner and beyond the horizon, enriching the meaning of every *aletheia*. And at every dimension of its organization, from local ecosystems to continent-spanning biomes, its processes and transformations can surprise with new events. To be sure, its surprises are not always the pleasant kind. Indeed some of its faces are dangerous. But nonetheless, even a short exploration of the Earth can prompt any number of aesthetic and religious pleasures, from the simple delight of spotting rabbit tracks in the snow where none had ever been seen before, all the way to world-encompassing moments of religious ecstasy. You might feel small and overwhelmed; you might feel amazed and delighted; you might feel welcomed and gathered in; and in any case, you might feel the event serves as a kind of partner in your search for answers to the highest and deepest questions.

My friends, there is a word for a fundamental reality capable of producing these experiences: *immensity*. In previous meditations we already found the material and phenomenological qualities which make the Earth an immensity: all but one. What remains is the question of its ethical authority. Does the Earth call to us? Does it summon us to action?

In at least one way, it does. As an Immensity, the presence of a grove of trees, a rushing stream, a bee-busy meadow, is the appearance of one or more possibilities for action, possibilities for being-free, for better or worse, and for those with the perception and initiative to pursue them. These possibilities are like a summons from the realm of the unseen, to grasp one or more of them and to make them into revealed realities. To take initiative is to respond to the summons. The test of the rightness of the response lies in the changed state of the Immensity, and the changed state of the person who faces it. The response is right when it opens possibilities for life-flourishing and life-enabling; it is wrong when it closes those possibilities or bends them toward life-diminishment and destruction.

This call may be hard to hear in the simple encounters: the beautiful meadow, the inspiring sunrise, the new stray weed in the garden. It is easier to hear when the Immensity fills a larger range of your field of view. The spectacle of a wide fertile valley, seen from a mountain top. The enclosing embrace of a forest, with its high canopy, its darting birds and smiling flowers, its rich earthy scents. The seemingly endless expanse of the ocean, especially as seen from sea cliffs and other great heights. The island of Inis Mór had such cliffs where the Immensity found me, no less powerful than the thunderstorm in Hessen which was for me a philosophical initiation. And although it may seem counter-intuitive, the summons also issues from the signs of climate crisis: the flood-damaged town, the fire-ravaged forest, the remnants of a meadow left brown and dead by a drought. These are like cries for help. This cry also flows from lands ploughed by Earth-moving machines and left in heaps of stone and mud, in preparation for a new housing development, a new confined-animal farm, or a new highway. Each event of this kind calls for a response. The right kind of response leads to increasing possibilities for continued *eudaimonia,* flourishing and happiness, the good and worthwhile life, for you and all your relations. The wrong kind decreases those possibilities.

To find the Immensity, we don't have to induce a sense of enchantment in some artificial or pretentious way. For the Immensity is always there. It always has been, and always will be. It isn't necessarily supernatural or mystical. We do not need to invent a new religion to find it. Indeed, it need not be an experience of 'enchantment' in the usual sense of the world – which is fine, since disenchantment itself is not the real problem. *The problem is that the circle of life is broken.* The Immensity is the phenomena which, standing in the place of Enchantment, calls upon us to heal the Circle, and in so doing, to heal ourselves and each other.

But is this perhaps only a cleverly disguised anthropocentrism? And did we not observe, not so long ago, that anthropocentrism could not save us – indeed, that it was part of the problem? Yes, the Call of the Earth as I have presented it so far is, at least in part, anthropocentric. For we must, of course, face the Immensity as free beings. Only a free being can choose to respond to the Earth with humanity, integrity, wonder, and any other virtues that lead to a worthwhile life. The chosen-ness of those virtues meets a need arising from our being-free. But that is only half of my point. There is an ecocentric dimension to the

Immensity as well. You can find it in the dialectic of call-and-response between the Earth and the person who faces it. Even as we face the Earth as free beings, we must also face it with a good understanding of its own processes and requirements, its own capacity for flourishing, its own life. This meets a need arising from our being-ecological: the need to participate in local and global ecosystems as a full partner in a life-affirming symbiosis.

System-complexity is the important quality here. It makes the *aletheia* of the Earth unpredictable, a fundamental reality governed by its own logic and its own lights, *and therefore impossible to possess*. The full argument runs as follows:

1.   The Earth is beautiful, a source of spiritual inspiration, a field of magic, and indeed our bio-physical life-support system, because (among other reasons) it is a complex system, a hyper-object, an immensity.

2.   We might relate to it by taking resources from it and depositing waste in return. That is to say, we might enclose some of its materials and lives into the human world, and take command of the functioning of its systems. We could, in principle, extend the reach of the enclosing until all things in its system are known, controlled, numbered, indexed, worked upon, and transformed into Things Of Man.

3.   But if we were to do that, the Earth *would no longer be a complex system*. It would be, instead, a mere object, an instrument, a stockpile of materials, an expression of the human spirit, and a field for the exercise of humanity's being-free.

4.   In that sense, the Earth *cannot be enclosed and stockpiled*. Or to be more precise: that quality about the Earth which makes it beautiful and spiritually inspiring, its Immensity, cannot be enclosed and stockpiled. The moment it is enclosed is also the moment it vanishes.

Like the mythical faerie-musician who inspires love in all those who hear her music, but who dies if she is captured and commanded to play, the Earth is a musician who dies in the same moment we try to call the tune.[241] This may obtain as a matter of degree; it need not be all-or-nothing.

5. The impossibility of enclosing and stockpiling the immensity of the Earth becomes, in ethics, a phenomenological demand for respect, and a summons to care.[242]

So let us sum up this meditation with another answer to my third root question. Can we heal the Circle of Life? *Yes – if we can dispel the illusion of infinite carrying capacity, escape the urban hyper-real, face the Immensity, hear its call, and respond to it with the right kinds of virtues, on multiple dimensions of human life and civilization.*

Therefore I propose:

• People need to be able to *see* what needs to be healed, and also see what the possibilities are for what a healed Circle of Life can look like. Therefore, every city on Earth should be surrounded and penetrated by green belts, bio-regeneration zones, and similar areas where the Immensity of Earth has not been entirely smothered by human design. It is perhaps unavoidable that a city park or a conservation area is designed, to some extent. But it must be possible for urban patches of nature to retain some of their magic, some of their capacity to surprise. If a park or a forest has been designed, organized, mapped, planned, and prepared, to the point where the Earth in that patch has no capacity to surprise, then its magic is entirely gone; its *aletheia* is all too human. But if there remains something about it which can still surprise even the designers and planners – if there remains enough of its spirit to make a visitor feel she has left the boundaries of the human world, even if only tentatively, like dipping a toe in the ocean – then it remains possible to break out of the urban hyper-real, even if only in some small way.

• All cities and national governments should adopt the 'doughnut economics' of Oxford professor Kate Raworth, or something close enough to it, in their planning policies. This is a model of economics which, resembling the principle of Sustainable Development, calls for a community's environmental impacts to remain within the boundaries of what the Earth can bear, and what is necessary for a decent standard of living for everyone. To transgress the ecological boundary is to overshoot; to transgress the social boundary is to fall short.[243] It's called 'doughnut economics' because the diagram to represent it is a circle with nine sectors, one for each of the social foundations featured in the UN Sustainable Development Goals.

• Asphalt-lands (roads and parking lots) in most residential and commercial neighbourhoods should be replaced with green space. Most cities today give between 35% and 50% of their land area to cars alone: that includes roads and parking lots.[244] Asphalt-lands cannot grow food, cannot have shade trees, cannot provide habitat for birds and wildlife, and cannot absorb rain water. They're dangerous to walk in, and dangerous for children to play in: it is as if cars have more human rights than people do. They concentrate the sun's heat and contribute to the creation of urban heat islands, making summer heat waves worse. *So rip them up!* Replace as much asphalt-land as possible with gardens, playgrounds, sports fields, hedgerows, trees, ponds, outdoor cafes, flood retention basins, and wildlife migration corridors. Keep one lane for deliveries, emergency vehicles, and public transit, but pave it with materials which capture less heat and which offer a more pleasing aesthetic. Re-zone residential neighbourhoods to allow small businesses and workshops at ground level, so people will not need to travel as far for work, shopping, cultural life, and the like. Install solar panel roofs over parking lots to keep them cool and to use the space more efficiently. In the near future, we will have less need for parking lots anyway, as people transition to car sharing, car rentals, bicycles, and electric scooters. There are numerous real-world models to follow here, including the Toronto Islands community, and the superblocks of Madrid.

If There Is Magic

I can hear the atheists and humanists among my friends saying: But the earth is indifferent to us. It has no mind, no consciousness, no deliberate intentionality. Symbiosis came to dominate its functions through billions of years of Darwinian trial-and-error, not through anyone's design. It happens to benefit us, as our biophysical life-support system. But it does this with no deliberate will. It sends us diseases, animal attacks, and destructive storms with exactly the same indifference. So there is no point in saying it 'calls' to us. The last of the Twelve Ways to Ecology expresses this indifference with great clarity: 'life goes on' whether we are part of it or not, and it will go on whether we human beings survive the crisis or not.

In reply, I wish to say: The indifference of the Earth is part of its Immensity, no less than Otherness is part of the Immensity of other people, inevitability is part of the Immensity of death; qualities which contribute to the way they, too, cannot be possessed, and thereby require from us excellence and justice. The indifference of the Earth makes it into a kind of Darwinian task-master, in which some human virtues fit with the state of things and so bring you closer to the good and worthwhile life, while others, which we must call vices, do not fit the reality, and so lead you further away. In that sense it might seem as if it's not the Earth who calls, but something within us which reaches out: something arising from our being-free. And that is not so bad. But we should face it according to its own being, its own *aletheia*, and not according to how we wish it was or imagine it to be. Thus the call arises from the special combination of our being-free, our being-ecological, the state of the Immensity when and where we face it, and the logical impossibility of possessing it without extinguishing its *aletheia*.

Others among my friends might say that magic is real. The earth is full of gods and spirits, and they give us reason enough to care for the Earth. They might feel invalidated by my argument that we should substitute Immensity in the place of Enchantment. For friends such as these, I wish to say: if there is magic out there in the world to be found, if the Earth is alive with its own spirit, *it is the right response to the Immensity which reveals it*. I'm suggesting here that magic, as a function of meaning, might be an emergent property of world, and that the right response to the Immensity creates the conditions for the possibility of its *aletheia*. It is as if the magic of the Earth dwells beyond the horizon of the unseen, and it calls to us to bring it forth into the realm of the seen.

In effect, this is a reversal of the usual argument for ecocentrism and enchantment. Instead of 'Let us protect the earth *because* it is magical,', I'm proposing 'Let us protect the earth *so that we may discover whether, where, and how,* it is magical; so that we may discover whether, where, and how the work of protecting it makes it magical.'

It might happen that the Earth is the dwelling-place of spirits who deserve our respect. It may happen that there are faeries, monsters, ghosts, and gods, living in my forest, and indeed living near you. It might be that we can gather magical energies from stones and trees and sunshine, to bless ourselves and others. It is sufficient, as a starting place, that the forest is full of life, and beautiful. Let us protect it so that we may discover more of its beauty, in whatever form that beauty takes, and so we may discover what more and what else its beauty entails.

Therefore I propose: the magic of the Earth and its life, if that magic is truly out there, will appear of its own accord, and without artificial prompting, if:

- in general, we make regular occasions to escape the urban hyper-real, to seek out and engage with the fundamental realities beneath it;
- on the personal level, we approach the Earth and all its life with more curiosity, wonder, playfulness, respect, care, gratitude, and love;
- on the level of local communities and cultures, we weaken the boundaries and injustices which led to disenchantment; and
- on the level of national and international economics and power-politics, we enforce clear limits to humanity's resource-extractions and pollution-outputs, engage in large-scale rewilding and bioremediation projects, and in general take up less space on the surface of the Earth.

Some people, following this plan as well as my other proposals, will not find the world more magical. But I hope that by following this plan anyway, they will find it more liveable, more interesting and pleasant, more supportive of their bodily health and their will to meaning, and also more just. We could thus revise the principle, to say: 'let us protect the Earth so we may discover whether, where, and how, the work of protecting it reveals better ways for us to live.' Again, it is as if innumerable possible worlds dwell beyond the horizon of the unseen, and the best of them summon us to bring them into *aletheia*, into revealed reality. A better world is a prize no less valuable than magic, and no less worth pursuing.

Plerosis

Green Sabbatical and Ecological Pilgrimage

We have come to the end of these meditations. We learned that the Immensity of Earth, and of the climate crisis, summons us to action in four different but related ways. First: the nature of the Immensity itself is such that the good life must be pursued in dialogue with it. Second: the breakdown of the Circle of Life ethically requires investigation and healing. Third: the impossibility of grasping or possessing the Immensity is, at the same time, an ethical demand to respect and to cooperate with it. And finally: the ethical necessity of healing the Circle of Life arises not from the belief that the Earth is magical, but rather from the promise that, in the course of the healing process, the Earth shall become magical. Or, if it does not become more magical, it certainly becomes more liveable, more just, and more beautiful.

I hope these ideas can constitute the foundation of a new human reality, in which we close the distance between our being-ecological and being-free, and find a healthier and more symbiotic relationship with the Earth. Or, to be more precise, they can be *the way we might go about both creating and discovering that new human reality*. Thus, if the quest did not end in the discovery of a treasure, it ended in the discovery of a path that leads to a treasure. And that, perhaps, is a treasure in its own right.

With that in mind, here are two more recommendations: two more signposts on the path. I think they are important enough to deserve meditations of their own, separate from the others. I hope you find them helpful.

First: choose one day a week, perhaps starting on a Friday evening and ending on the Saturday evening, to take a *Green Sabbatical*.

It's a day in which you turn off all digital devices, do not watch television or consume any digital mass-market media of any kind, do not take overtime at your job, spend no money, and do not drive your car. Instead, give the time to renewing and enriching your relationships with your people and your local ecosystem. Make art and music and food, with and for your family and friends. Play with children. Explore a park. Plant a garden. Go camping and hiking. Play sports and games. Host a philosophical salon or a poetry recital. Practice a new hobby or handicraft. Meditate. Sleep in late in the morning. Read a book. "Dance, sing, feast, make music, and love" with your partner and your intimates.[245] Talk to each other! If you must travel during this time, plan it in advance, and take public transit. I have in mind here a focused version of the Jewish practice of *shabbat*, in which conservative and orthodox Jews do no work of any kind from sundown Friday to sundown Saturday. The aim of a Green Sabbatical is threefold: to lighten your footprint upon the Earth; to seek out the immensities in your world, including in the people around you; and to include them in activities that affirm the goodness and beauty of life.

Second: I propose that once a year, or more often, if possible, everyone should undertake an *Ecological Pilgrimage*.

I'm partly inspired here by a custom, popular among young people in my hometown, to go up to northern Ontario for the summer to plant trees in areas recently harvested by logging companies. (Well, this custom ended in the 1990s, when the oil patch in Alberta offered better paying and more permanent jobs.) Many people did it out of a sense of environmental responsibility. Probably most people did it for the adventure, the money, and the chance to get away from their parents. I'm proposing here that we do something similar, but not as an 'escape', nor as a working holiday, nor as a vacation, nor as something only the young can do. I propose the Ecological Pilgrimage as a kind of *sacred quest* to a place where you can see the Circle of Life spread out before you, and to hear its call. I'm using religious language here, even though humanists and atheists could adopt this practice with no trouble. It is a *philosophical-spiritual* activity, in the sense that it brings together your being-ecological with your being-free, and in the sense that it involves pursuing an encounter with the Immensity.

The Green Pilgrimage begins with the choice of a destination. It should be somewhere mostly wild: some place where the Immensity of Earth is as little contained by the urban hyper-real as possible. Conservation parks, national forests, wildlife refuges insofar as visitors are allowed, and the like, are good choices here. If there are no such destinations within your reach, it can be part of your Pilgrimage to lobby your government to create them. If you find others around you wishing to make their own Pilgrimage but for some reason they cannot, it can be part of your Pilgrimage to empower them so that they can. Your destination should also be some place where the means of travel involves some friction: that is, some of the journey must be taken on foot, on horseback, by canoe, by bicycle (that is to say, *not* by a motorized vehicle), and over terrain that tests your body's endurance. It should take all day to get there; perhaps even several days. Each pilgrim, or party of pilgrims, should choose a place that is neither impossible nor too easy, in accord with their abilities; thus a person with a mobility-impairment might choose a destination with wide roads, while someone with no disabilities might choose a destination with rough and narrow trails. The idea is to make the pilgrimage *effortful*, and so to create a deserved sense of accomplishment and proper pride.

Importantly, your destination should be a place where you can find a view of the world with as little sign of the human realm as possible. No power lines, no houses, no highways, no noise from machines, no farms. A place where the Immensity fills as much of your field of view as possible. Or, a place that has some kind of personal, poetic, or historical sacredness for you. The sacred, let me remind you, is that which acts as your partner in your search for the highest and deepest things: the good, the real, the true, and the beautiful. Choose a destination for your pilgrimage which might awaken that search in your body, heart, and mind.

You can bring friends, and you can bring whatever supplies and equipment you need, including your cellphone in case you need to call for help (but keep it turned off most of the time). Indeed, bringing friends can enhance the sense of being on a quest: the adventure, the effort needed, and the accomplishment, when shared, creates social bonds of friendship and love that can last for years.

When you reach your destination, remain for at least three full days. Go into the forest and seek its heart, look for it, listen for it, touch it, breathe it. Let it speak to you in its own way. Let it be a little dangerous, if that is how it needs to go. Remember that you are a pilgrim here: go in the manner of a small and fragile being in search of belonging and blessing.

At some point during the pilgrimage, there are three propositions to meditate upon. Look to the forest and say to yourself: *This is greater than me; this shall always be greater than me.* Grasp that greatness; feel your smallness next to it; let it fold into your sense of self-worth. You might find, as astronomers and theologians sometimes find when they contemplate their respective immensities, and as astronauts find when they meet the overview effect, that the problems of politics and economics and human tribal competitions are of no importance, no great urgency, *sub specie aeternitatis*, under the aspect of eternity. This feeling of smallness has surprising psychological benefits including the stimulation of empathy, pro-social behaviour, and (though it may seem counter-intuitive) a greater sense of life-satisfaction.[246]

Then look again and say to yourself: *This gives life to me; this is always empowering and preserving me.* Grasp that relationship; feel your intimacy with it; let it fold into your sense of being-ecological and your sense of self-worth. Ecosystems and biomes and all the lives within them, all over the world, are keeping you alive. You may find this proposition makes other people feel closer to you. For they, too, are borne of the same Earth; they too are sustained and preserved by it. You share the same atmosphere, the same ocean, the same Circle of Life, with every human in the world today, and every human who has ever lived. This is one way to realise how everything you do affects someone somewhere, and how we always have more in common with strangers than we have in contrast.

Then look a third time and say: *This needs me; this will always need me.* It needs your complete and undivided attention. It needs your care and concern. Its organic functions and ecological circles need your cooperation. It needs your protection from others who, in their ignorance or their hubris, have not yet grasped the nature of the crisis. It needs your intelligence; it needs you to understand its functions and its characters. It needs your will to power. It needs your will to love.

These three propositions need not be 'affirmations' in the religious sense. They are factual and experiential propositions designed to convey the meaning of your participation in the Circle of Life. Whisper them or dream them, if you feel embarrassed to utter them out loud. Sing them or pray them, if the moment so moves you. But in any case, think about them, while you look to the world, and think about what follows from them.

It is possible that none of my suggestions will be enough to heal the Circle of Life. We have people among us who will never feel any love for the Earth. Some people will go on this Green Pilgrimage and yet remain committed to the illusion of infinite carrying capacity. Some will continue to believe that we will all be saved from the climate crisis by God, or by some technology that has not yet been invented. Some will wish they were back home, immersed in the urban hyper-real again. Some will continue to believe that other problems deserve more attention. But I hope that *enough* people will come to be inspired by the Immensity of the Earth to want to help and protect it.

This leads to a final answer to the third root question. Can we heal the Circle of Life: *Yes – if enough people come to love the Earth, to hear its call, to grasp what needs to be done, and do it.*

References

1. David Yaden, Jonathan Iwry, et.al., "The Overview Effect: Awe and Self-Transcendent Experience in Space Flight" *Psychology of Consciousness*, Vol.3, No.1, 2016, pp. 1-11.

2. S. Chen, *A documentary on Shenzhou-9* (Hunan, China: The Science and Technology Press of Hunan, 2012), pg. 288.

3. F. White, *The overview effect: Space exploration and human evolution*. (Boston: Houghton Mifflin, 1987) pg.12.

4. R. Jaffe, *Anthropogenic relation to other biota: Connections to disorders and crisis of our time*. (Ashburn, VA, USA: Health Studies Collegium, 2011) pg. 9.

5. Phoebe Weston, "Birds 'falling out of the sky' in mass die-off in south-western US" *The Guardian*, 16 September 2020.

6. Daniel Becker, Indiana University, cited in Maira Ansari, "Birds dying in Indiana and Kentucky remains a mystery" *WVLT Knoxville, TN*. 26th June 2021.

7. I. Newton, Weather-related mass-mortality events in migrants. Ibis: International Journal of Avian Science, Vol.149, Iss.3 (May 2007), pp. 453-467.

8. See, for example: International Panel on Climate Change: *Global Warming of 1.5°C. An IPCC Special Report on the impacts of global warming of 1.5°C above pre-industrial levels and related global greenhouse gas emission pathways, in the context of strengthening the global response to the threat of climate change, sustainable development, and efforts to eradicate poverty*. [Masson-Delmotte, V., P. Zhai, H.-O. Pörtner, et al. (eds.)]. Cambridge University Press, 2018.

9. International Panel on Climate Change: "Summary for Policymakers." In: *Climate Change 2021: The Physical Science Basis. Contribution of Working Group I to the Sixth Assessment Report of the Intergovernmental Panel on Climate Change* [Masson-Delmotte, V., P. Zhai, A. Pirani, S. L.

Connors, et.al. (eds.)]. Cambridge University Press, 2021.

10. Doreen Valiente, "The Charge of the Goddess". This short text composed by Valiente in 1954 serves as one of the foundational sacred texts of the neo-Pagan movement (if, indeed, it has a body of 'texts' at all).

11. International Panel on Climate Change, 2018: pg. 54.

12. Jeff Dillon, *Another Climate Milestone Falls at Mauna Loa Observatory* (Press release from The Scripps Institution of Oceanography, UC San Diego, 7th June 2018.)

13. *CO2 at NOAA's Mauna Loa Observatory reaches new milestone: Tops 400 ppm* (Press release from Global Monitoring Division, Earth System Research Laboratory, United States National Oceanographic and Atmospheric Administration, 10th May 2013.)

14. For a complete accounting of the anti-science forces and their corporate financial backers, see Michael Mann, *The New Climate War* (New York: Hachette Book Group, 2021). Dr. Mann is a professor of atmospheric sciences at Penn State University, and a recipient of the Tyler Prize for Environmental Achievement.

15. Edward L. Rubin, "Rejecting Climate Change: Not Science Denial, but Regulation Phobia" *Journal of Land Use and Environmental Law*, Vol.32, Is.1, Fall 2016, pp. 103-150.

16. Staff writers, "Storms and fires will not bring an escape from America's stuck climate politics." *The Economist*. 4th September 2021.

17. Cited in Pittis, "What you can do in 2020 to keep the world from burning up", *CBC News*, 30 December 2019.

18. Leopold, *A Sand County Almanac*, cited in Botzler and Armstrong, *Environmental Ethics; Divergence and Convergence*. (Boston: McGraw Hill, 1998) pg., 413.

19. Leopold, *ibid*, pg. 412-3.

20. Albert Schweitzer, *The Philosophy Of Civilization, Vol.2: Civilization And Ethics*, translated by C. Campion, 3rd

[English] Edition. (London: Adam & Charles Black, 1955.), pg. 242.

21. Schweitzer, *ibid*, pg. 243-4.

22. Hans Jonas, *The Phenomenon of Life* (Evanston, Illinois, USA: Northwestern University Press, 2001 [first published 1966]), pg. 46.

23. The distinction is subtle, but important. A complicated system is one with many parts and functions, but there is nothing about the system or its parts which is intrinsically incomprehensible. A *complex* system is one where the nature of the system produces effects, or properties, which are not predictable from knowledge of the system's parts.

24. Hava Tirosh-Samuelson and Christian Wiese, eds., *The Legacy of Hans Jonas: Judaism and the Phenomenon of Life* (Brill, 2008), pg. 135.

25. Jonas, *ibid*, pg. 284.

26. Charles A. Reich, *The Greening of America* (New York: Random House, 1970 / Bantam, 1971), pp.7-8.

27. *ibid.*, pp. 259, 275-6.

28. Lynn White, Jr., "The Historical Roots of Our Ecological Crisis" *Science*, Vol.155 (1967), pp. 1203-1207.

29. Arne Naess, "The Deep Ecology Movement: Some Philosophical Aspects" *Philosophical Inquiry*, Vol.8 (1986), pp. 10-31.

30. McMurtry, *Unequal Freedoms: The Global Market as an Ethical System* (Garamond, 1998) p. 6.

31. Paul Taylor, *Respect for Nature* Princeton University Press, 1986), pg. 129.

32. The World Commission on Environment and Development / The Brundtland Commission. *Our Common Future.* (Oxford University Press, 1987) pg. 43.

33. "But just this uncertainty, which threatens to make the ethical insight ineffectual for the long-range responsibility toward the future... has itself to be included in the ethical

theory and become the cause of a new principle, which on its part can yield a not uncertain rule for decision-making. It is the rule, stated primitively, that the prophesy of doom is to be given greater heed than the prophesy of bliss." Hans Jonas, *The Imperative of Responsibility: In Search of Ethics for the Technological Age* (University of Chicago Press, 1984), pg. 31. [translation of *Das Prinzip Verantwortung,* first published 1979]).

34. Raffensperger and Tickner, *Protecting Public Health and the Environment: Implementing the Precautionary Principle* (Washington DC USA: Island Press, 1999) pg.8.

35. I acknowledge the inspiration of Swedish climate activist Greta Thunberg, whose general message follows the same logical structure. 1) If politicians and industrialists were doing enough, then the climate crisis would slow down or abate. 2) The climate crisis has not slowed down nor abated. 3) It follows that politicians and industrialists are not doing enough.

36. J. McMurtry, *Unequal Freedoms: The Global Market as an Ethical System* (Toronto: Garamond, 1998) pg. 164.

37. Sarah Pulliam Bailey, "Why so many evangelicals in Trump's base are deeply skeptical of climate change" *The Washington Post,* 2nd June 2017.

38. Lisa Vox, "Why don't Christian conservatives worry about climate change? God." *The Washington Post,* 2nd June 2017.

39. Pope Francis, *Encyclical On Climate Change And Inequality.* (New York: Melville House, 2015).

40. Eric McDaniel, "Pope Francis And Other Christian Leaders Are Calling For Bold Climate Action". *NPR,* 10th September 2021.

41. Eric McDaniel, *ibid,* for Archbishop Justin Welby; Staff writers, "God 'will not give happy ending'', *BBC News,* 26th March 2009, for Archbishop Rowan Williams.

42. Cristina Maza, "Trump will start the end of the world,

claim evangelicals who support him" *Newsweek*, 1st December 2018.

43. Andrea Lobel, PhD, a rabbi in the tradition of Jewish Renewal (and my partner), informs me that the verses about justice are among the central themes of the Hebrew Bible. Further, in the Hebrew Bible and in Rabbinic literature, it is clear that concepts of stewardship of the Earth have high priority.

44. Irene Mecchi, Jonathan Roberts, and Linda Wooverton, screenwriters: *The Lion King* (Disney, 1994).

45. Andrew Brennan, *Thinking about Nature: An Investigation of Nature, Value and Ecology* (Routledge, 2014 [first edition 1988]) pg. 45.

46. Cited in: F. Egerton, *Roots of Ecology: Antiquity to Haekel* (Berkeley, California: U of California Press, 2012) Original publication: London: W. Mears, 1721, ch.XIV pg. 159.

47. Forbes, "The Lake as a Microcosm", *Bulletin of the Scientific Association* (Peoria, IL, USA, 1887) pp.77-87.

48. Forbes, *ibid*, pg. 86.

49. Forbes, *ibid*, pg. 86; emphasis his.

50. Forbes, *ibid*, pg. 87.

51. Forbes, "On Some Interactions of Organisms", *Bulletin of the Illinois State Laboratory of Natural History*, Vol.1, No.3 (1880)

52. William Paley, *Natural Theology* (Boston: Gould and Lincoln, 1867 [first published 1802]) pg.13.

53. Clements, F.E. *Research Methods in Ecology* (Lincoln Nebraska USA: University Publishing Co., 1905) pg. 265.

54. C. S. Elton, *Animal Ecology and Evolution* (Oxford University Press, New York, 1930); see also Sharon Kingsland, *Modelling Nature: Episodes in the History of Population Ecology* (University of Chicago Press, Chicago USA, 1985)

55. Bethany Lindsay and Courtney Dickson, "Village of Lytton, BC., evacuated as mayor says 'the whole town is

on fire'" *CBC News*, 30th June 2021; Rhianna Schmunk, "'Most homes' in Lytton, B.C., destroyed by catastrophic fire, minister says" *CBC News*, 1st July 2021.

56. Jason Horowitz, "A Sicilian Town Sends an Omen of a Much Hotter Future" *The New York Times*, 13 August 2021.

57. Adam Vaughan, "Life found beneath Antarctic ice sheet 'shouldn't be there'" *New Scientist*, 15th February 2021.

58. Jonathan Watts, "Scientists identify vast underground ecosystem containing billions of micro-organisms" *The Guardian*, 10th December 2018.

59. Michael Polyani, "Life's Irreducible Structure: Live mechanisms and information in DNA are boundary conditions with a sequence of boundaries above them" *Science*, 21 June 1968, Vol.160, Iss.3834, pp. 1308-1312.

60. Ferris Jabr, "How brainless slime moulds redefine intelligence" *Nature,* 13th November 2012.

61. Scott Turner, J. "Ventilation and thermal constancy of a colony of a southern African termite (Odontotermes transvaalensis: Macrotermitinae)". *Journal of Arid Environments*. 28(3), November 1994. pp 231-248.

62. I'm partly inspired by Barry Commoner's four "laws of ecology": 1) Everything is connected to everything else, 2) Everything must go somewhere, 3) Nature knows best, and 4) There is no such thing as a free lunch. But I have never found his laws entirely satisfying. To me, it seems they owe more to Commoner's rhetorical cleverness than to observable reality.

63. For instance, the jellyfish *Turritopsis dohrnii* may actually be immortal. When it is injured or old, it can revert its cells to their polyp stage, and so begin its life anew. See, for instance, Nathaniel Rich, "Can a jellyfish unlock the secret of immortality?". *The New York Times Magazine*, 28 November 2012.

64. Michael Crichton, *Jurassic Park* (New York: Ballantine,

1990 / 2015) pg. 179.

65. Darwin's own views on that point are somewhat ambiguous. In *The Origin of Species,* he said, "there should be open competition for all men; and the most able should not be prevented by laws from succeeding best and rearing the largest number of offspring". Yet in the same text, some hundred pages later, he also says "the moral qualities are advanced... much more through the effects of habit, the reasoning powers, instruction, religion, etc., than through natural selection." Charles Darwin, *On the Origin of Species,* pp. 304, 404.

66. Spottiswoode, C., Begg, K. S., & Begg, C. M. (2016). "Reciprocal signalling in honeyguide-human mutualism." *Science,* Vol.353, pp.387-389. There is some evidence that honeyguides also cooperate with other animals, such as badgers. But this evidence is inconclusive at this time.

67. Brad Bulin, "Naturalist Notes: Wolves and Ravens" *Yellowstone Quarterly,* 10th March 2020. I am also grateful to Melinda Reidinger for drawing my attention to this relationship.

68. Margulis, *The Symbiotic Planet* (London: Phoenix / Orion, 1998 [reissue of 2001]), pg. 15.

69. Suzanne Simard, *Finding the Mother Tree* (New York: Random House, 2021). Page number refers to the large-print edition; I don't know why the publisher sent me that one instead of a normal one.

70. W. Ripple and R. Beschta, "Trophic cascades in Yellowstone: The first 15 years after wolf reintroduction" *Biological Conservation,* Vol. 145, Iss.2, January 2012, pp. 205-213; Ripple, Beschta, Fortin, and Robbins, "Trophic cascades from wolves to grizzly bears in Yellowstone" *Journal of Animal Ecology* 83(1), pp. 223-233; G. Monbiot, *Feral: Rewilding the Land, Sea, and Human Life* (London: Penguin, 2013) pp. 84-5.

71. Ripple and Beschta, "Linking Wolves and Plants: Aldo Leopold on Trophic Cascades" *Bioscience* 55(7), pp. 613-621.

72. In case you're curious, the energy is radiated out as light with a frequency equal to the fourth power of the system's average temperature, times the Stefan-Boltzmann constant. The equation looks like this: Power output = the surface area of the object $\times$ (kT^4). But don't worry about the mathematics. The main takeaway is that as more energy goes in, the system radiates the energy out as light with an increasingly higher frequency.

73. James Lovelock, *The Ages of Gaia* (W.W. Norton, New York, 1990) pg. 19.

74. The ability of living systems to defy entropy in this way was explained by Canadian physicists Eric Schneider and James Kay in 1994, through a reformulation of the entropy law. They defined it as follows: as systems are "…moved away from equilibrium, they will utilise all avenues available to counter applied gradients [external sources of energy]. As applied gradients increase, so does a system's ability to oppose further movement from equilibrium." Schneider and Kay, "Life as a Manifestation of the Second Law of Thermodynamics" *Mathematical and Computer Modelling* Vol. 18 No 6-8, March-April 1994, pg. 31.

75. Schneider & Kay, *ibid*, pg. 32.

76. Schneider & Kay, *ibid*, pg. 40.

77. See: Stuart Kauffman, *At Home In The Universe: The Search for the Laws of Self-Organization and Complexity*, Revised edition. (Oxford University Press, 1996). See also: "The Adjacent Possible: A Talk With Stuart A. Kauffman" *Edge*, 9th November 2003.

78. This also helps to explain why there is more biodiversity in the tropics than in other latitudes. The tropics receive more solar radiation, requiring tropical ecosystems to find

ways to disperse the greater volume of energy. The tropics also have fewer climactic differences between summer and winter, and the days and nights are of more equal length. Both of these conditions produce more ecological niches, allowing populations of organisms to specialize and so to speciate; this also produces more competition for the available niches.

79. In engineering, this is called elastic deformation and plastic deformation.

80. Laurence Krauss, *The Physics of Climate Change* (New York: Post Hill Press, 2021), pg. 33.

81. Thornalley, D.J.R., Oppo, D.W., Ortega, P. *et al.* "Anomalously weak Labrador Sea convection and Atlantic overturning during the past 150 years." *Nature,* Vol.556 (2018), pp. 227-230; Boers, N. "Observation-based early-warning signals for a collapse of the Atlantic Meridional Overturning Circulation." *Nature Climate Change.* **11,** 680-688 (2021); J. Hansen, M. Sato, P. Hearty, R. Ruedy, M. Kelley, V. Masson-Delmotte, G. Russell, G. Tselioudis, J. Cao, E. Rignot, I. Velicogna, E. Kandiano, K. von Schuckmann, P. Kharecha, A. N. Legrande, M. Bauer, and K.-W. Lo (2015). "Ice melt, sea level rise and superstorms: evidence from paleoclimate data, climate modeling, and modern observations that 2 °C global warming is highly dangerous". *Atmospheric Chemistry and Physics Discussions.* 15 (14): 20059-20179

82. Henry Fountain, "Researchers Link Syrian Conflict to a Drought Made Worse by Climate Change" *The New York Times,* 2nd March 2015.

83. Though it is my usual habit to avoid gendered nouns where possible, here I think the male pronoun is appropriate, since it is mostly men, and relatively few women, who own and command the forces of civilization: its economics, its politics, its religions, its means of communication, and so

on. This is an observable, mathematically quantifiable fact and deserves greater public acknowledgement; evaluate its moral significance as you will.

84. *Imagined*, in the sense of an *image*, a picture, even a reflection; but not in the sense of something made up out of nothing, like a fantasy.

85. Roddenberry, Nimoy, and Bennett, screenwriters. *Star Trek: The Voyage Home* (Paramount, 1986)

86. For a full treatment of that outrageous statement, see Myers, *Reclaiming Civilization* (Moon Books, 2017), pp. 183-215.

87. Timothy Morton, *Hyperobjects: Philosophy and Ecology after the End of the World* (University of Minnesota Press, 2013), pg. 1. See also Morton, *The Ecological Thought* (Harvard University Press, 2012), where Morton introduced the idea of the hyperobject for the first time. (As an aside, I published my concept of Immensity for the first time in 2008, which is one reason why I continue to use it here.)

88. *ibid*, pp. 31-2.

89. *ibid, pg. 47.*

90. *ibid*, pg. 60.

91. *ibid*, pp. 1-2.

92. I acknowledge the inspiration of climate researcher Prof. Sandra Steingraber on these points. Cf: Steingraber, "Commentary: A farewell to Ithaca College after 18 years" *The Ithacan* (Ithaca, NY), 9th March 2021.

93. Beyer, Manica, and Mora. "Shifts in global bat diversity suggest a possible role of climate change in the emergence of SARS-CoV-1 and SARS CoV-2." *Science of the Total Environment*, 26 January 2021, 145413.

94. There may also have been intermediate hosts, such as pangolins or other animals attacked by bats and later sold at wet-markets and eaten by people. See: Scripps Research Institute. "COVID-19 coronavirus epidemic

has a natural origin." *ScienceDaily*. www.sciencedaily. com/releases/2020/03/200317175442.htm (accessed June 18, 2020); Katarina Zimmer, "Deforestation is leading to more infectious diseases in humans" *National Geographic*, 22 November 2019; John Vidal, Ensia, "Destroyed habitat creates the perfect conditions for Coronavirus to emerge" *Scientific American*, 18 March 2020.

95. "The coronavirus may not have originated in China, says Oxford professor" *BBC Science Focus Magazine*, 6th July 2020.

96. "Climate change and human health: risks and responses. Summary." *World Health Organization*, 2003.

97. Afelt, Frutos, & Devaux, "Bats, Coronaviruses, and Deforestation: Toward the emergence of novel infectious diseases?" *Frontiers in Microbiology*, 11 April 2018.

98. Colin Barras, "We know the city where HIV first emerged" *BBC Earth*, 19 November 2015; see also: Sharp & Hahn, "Origins of HIV and the AIDS Pandemic" *Cold Spring Harbor Perspectives in Medicine*, Vol.1, No.1, September 2011.

99. For a complete treatment of the ethical dimension of the Immensity, see Myers, *The Other Side of Virtue* (O Books, 2008), pp. 154-238, and also Myers, *Circles of Meaning, Labyrinths of Fear* (Moon Books, 2010).

100. See: Stephen Cave, *Immortality: The quest to live forever and how it drives civilization* (New York: Crown, 2012).

101. Walter Pichler and Hans Hollein, "Absolute Architecture", in *Programs and Manifestos on 20th Century Architecture,* ed. Ulrich Conrads, trans. Michael Bullock. (Cambridge: MIT Press, 1975) pg. 181.

102. For commentary remarks on Hollein's manifesto, see Karsten Harries, *The Ethical Function of Architecture* (MIT Press, 1997) pg. 237.

103. Le Corbusier, *Towards a New Architecture*, trans. Frederick

Etchells (New York: Praeger, 1960), 65-66.

104. Karsten Harries, *ibid*, pg. 151.

105. Harries, *ibid*, pg. 303.

106. Harries, *ibid*, pg. 231.

107. Heidegger, *Being And Time*, trans. Maquarrie and Robinson (London: Blackwell, 1962) H.135, pg. 174.

108. *Being And Time*, H.284, pg. 329.

109. "With Dasein's factical existence, entities within-the-world are already encountered too. The fact that such entities are discovered along with Dasein's own "there" of existence, is not left to Dasein's discretion. Only *what* it discovers and discloses on occasion, in *what* direction it does so, *how* and *how far* it does so – only these are matters for Dasein's freedom, even if always within the limitations of its thrownness." *Being And Time*, H.366.

110. "The more authentically Dasein resolves [to accept its fate, death] – and this means that in anticipating death it understands itself unambiguously in terms of its ownmost distinctive possibility – the more unequivocally does it choose and find the possibility of its existence, and the less does it do so by accident. Only by the anticipation of death is every accidental and 'provisional' possibility driven out. Only being free *for* death, gives Dasein is goal outright and pushes its existence into its finitude... This is how we designate Dasein's primordial historizing, which lies in authentic resoluteness and in which Dasein *hands* itself *down* to itself, free for death, in a possibility which it has inherited and yet has chosen." *Being And Time*, H.383-4, pg. 435.

111. Levinas, *Time And the Other*, pp. 71-2.

112. Lévinas, *ibid*, 73.

113. Nietzsche, *Thus Spoke Zarathustra* ("The Drunken Song", §10), cited in *The Portable Nietzsche,* trans. W. Kaufman (Penguin, 1954) pg. 435.

114. In my childhood and youth, and through most of my twenties, I had the ability to detect magnetic north. Most people in my life did not believe me. Some friends of mine and I conducted experiments and found that after being spun around in a circle blindfolded, I could point towards magnetic north, within a 30-degree margin of error, on average four times out of five. I no longer possess this ability. Perhaps I am getting older, perhaps my body has grown accustomed to being immersed in the radio waves broadcasting from home WIFI routers. But magneto-detection is already well established in the animal kingdom, and there is some interesting (though still inconclusive) scientific research showing that at least *some* humans can, indeed, detect the Earth's magnetic field. See, for example: Wang, Hilburn, Mizuhara, et.al., "Transduction of the Geomagnetic Field as Evidence from alpha-Band Activity in the Human Brain" *eNeuro*, an open-access journal of the Society for Neuroscience, 18th March 2019, Vol.6, No.2.

115. I first introduced the concept of perceptual intelligence in *Circles of Meaning, Labyrinths of Fear* (Moon Books, 2010),

116. R. Ross, *Dancing with a Ghost: Exploring Indian Reality* (Markham, Ontario, Canada: Octopus Publishing Group, 1992) pg. 70.

117. Ross, *Ibid.*, pg. 72-3.

118. Ross, *ibid*, pg. 74.

119. Davis, *The Wayfinders*, pg. 59.

120. Sabine Wendler, "Biological diversity evokes happiness: More bird species in their vicinity increase life satisfaction of Europeans as much as higher income" Press release, Senckenberg Biodiversität und Klima Forschungszentrum, Gothe-Universität Frankfurt and Helmut-Schmidt Universität Hamburg, 4th December 2020; Methorst, Rehdanz, Mueller, et.al., "The importance of species

diversity for human well-being in Europe" *Ecological Economics*, Vol.181, 106917 (March 2021).

121. Sturm, Datta, Roy, et.al., "Big smile, small self: Awe walks promote positive emotions in older adults" *Emotion*, 21 September 2020.

122. Virginia Sturm, PhD, professor of neuroscience at UCSF, cited in Nicholas Weiler, "'Awe Walks' Boost Emotional Well-Being" *UCSF Research*, 21 September 2020.

123. David Leavens, "The Pointing Ape", *Aeon Magazine*, 1st October 2019; Butterworth, G., & Grover, L., "The origins of referential communication in human infancy." In L. Weiskrantz (Ed.), *A Fyssen Foundation symposium. Thought without language.* (Clarendon Press/Oxford University Press, 1988) pp. 5-24.

124. Karsten Harries, *The Ethical Function of Architecture* (MIT Press, 1997) pg. 139.

125. Abram, *The Spell of the Sensuous* (New York: Penguin, 1996), pg. 140.

126. E.S. Morton, "Ecological sources of selection on avian sounds." *The American Naturalist.* Vol. 109, No. 965 (1975), pp. 17-34.

127. Abram, *ibid*, pg. 145.

128. Abram, *ibid*, pg. 147-8.

129. Arne Naess, "The Deep Ecology Movement: Some Philosophical Aspects" *Philosophical Inquiry*, Vol.8 No.1-2 (1986), 10-31.

130. See for example Wolfgang Köhler, *Gestalt Psychology* (1947).

131. Domicele Jonauskaite, Ahmad Abu-Akel, Nele Dael, et.al., "Universal Patterns in Color-Emotion Associations Are Further Shaped by Linguistic and Geographic Proximity". *Psychological Science*, 31(10), Oct 2020, epub on 8th Sept. 2020.

132. Nelson and Simmons, "On Southbound Ease and

Northbound Fees: Literal Consequences of the Metaphoric Link between Vertical Position and Cardinal Direction" *Journal of Marketing Research*, 15 February 2007 (revised 8th May 2012).

133. Varda Liberman, et.al., "The Name of the Game: Predictive Power of Reputations versus Situational Labels in Determining Prisoner's Dilemma Game Moves" *Personality and Social Psychology Bulletin*, 30(9), 1st September 2004, pp. 1175-85.

134. Ravens, goldfinches, and grackles.

135. Alison Flood, "Oxford Junior Dictionary's replacement of 'natural' words sparks outcry" *The Guardian*, 13 January 2015; Robert McFarlane and Jackie Morris, *The Lost Words* (Toronto, Canada: House of Anansi Press, 2018).

136. Robert Macfarlane, "The word-hoard: Robert Macfarlane on rewilding our language of landscape" *The Guardian*, 27 February 2015.

137. Julie Henry, "Words associated with Christianity and British history taken out of children's dictionary" *The Telegraph*, 6th December 2008.

138. Natural England / England Marketing, "Report to Natural England on Childhood and Nature: A Survey on Changing Relationships With Nature Across Generations". *Natural England*, March 2009.

139. Masashi Soga, et.al., "How can we mitigate against increasing biophobia among children during the extinction of experience?" *Biological Conservation*, Vol.242, February 2020.

140. For this list, I acknowledge the inspiration of stand-up philosopher George Carlin's research on "soft language". Cf. Carlin, *Parental Advisory: Explicit Lyrics* (Atlantic Records, 1990).

141. For this list, I acknowledge the inspiration of journalist and environmental policy analyst George Monbiot's op-ed

essay: "Forget 'the environment': we need new words to convey life's wonders" *The Guardian*, 9th August 2017.

142. C.f. Myers, *Reclaiming Civilization* (Moon Books, 2017), chapter 28.

143. *Autobiography of William Carlos William,* cited in Felstiner, John. "A Selection from So Much Depends: Poetry and Environmental Urgency." *The American Poetry Review* 36, no. 1 (2007): 11-15.

144. Deborah Schein, "Nature's Role in Children's Spiritual Development" Colorado University: *Children, Youth, and Environments.* Vol, 24 No. 2 (2014), 78-101.

145. Rousseau, *Emile, or On Education,* trans. Allan Bloom (Basic Books, 1979), pg. 79. Emphasis added.

146. Rousseau, *Emile,* pg. 90.

147. Rousseau, *Emile,* pg. 95.

148. White, E. J. "Seeing is Believing? Insights from young children in nature." *International Journal of Early Childhood, Vol.*47 (2015), 171-188.

149. P. Aslanimehr, E. Marsal, B. Weber, F. Knapp, "Nature gives and nature takes: a qualitative comparison between Canadian and German children about their concepts of 'nature'" *Childhood and Philosophy*, v.14. no.30, May 2018, pp. 483-515.

150. As adults we do not treat even sex as an intrinsic good: we do it for the sake of satiating a need, or even a hunger; we do it for the sake of emotional bonding and the maintenance of relationships; we do it to conceive children; we do it as a duty to God and our partners. We encircle it with rules about who you may have sex with, and when, and what kind of sex you can and cannot have. There are good reasons for *some* of these rules – the ones about consent and safety and equality, for instance – but I'm sure you can see my point. Some of the rules transform a private act of intimacy into an occasion to affirm or to subvert public

religious or political values.

151. K. Groos, *The play of animals* (New York: Appleton, 1898); Groos, *The play of man* (New York: Appleton, 1901); Jean Piaget, *Play, dreams, and imitation* (New York: Norton, 1962).

152. See, for example, Shonkoff JP, Phillips DA, eds. *From Neurons to Neighborhoods: The Science of Early Childhood Development.* Washington, DC: National Academy Press, 2000; Hurwitz SC., "To be successful: let them play!" *Child Education,*2002/2003;79 :101-102; Barnett LA., "Developmental benefits of play for children." *J Leis Res.*1990;22 :138-153; Pellegrini AD, Smith PK., "The development of play during childhood: forms and possible functions." *Child Psychology and Psychiatry Review,* 998;3 :51-57

153. Rubin, K. H., Fein, G., & Vandenberg, B. "Play". In E. M. Hetherington (Ed.), *Handbook of child psychology: Socialization, personality, and social development, Vol IV.* (New York: Wiley, 1983) pp.693-774.

154. Pellegrini, Anthony D.; Smith, Peter K., "The Development of Play During Childhood: Forms and Possible Functions" *Child & Adolescent Mental Health.* May 1998, Vol. 3 Issue 2, pp. 51-57.

155. Many of my associates and friends will be disappointed by the proposition that magic is a function of meaning. They might say: 'But what about divine inspirations, spirit communications, psychic phenomena, prophetic dreams, and paranormal experiences? A large number of non-fools have had such experiences, so there must be something to them.' To this I have to reply: I have had many spiritual experiences in my life, but none of them were *supernatural* or *paranormal* as such. This of course doesn't mean such things aren't real. But it does mean that I have to make my argument as sound and strong as I can whether or not that

kind of magic is real. Further: the urgency and seriousness of the climate crisis is such that the moral necessity to face the crisis must be made obvious to everyone, magic-believers and the disenchanted alike.

156. Fein, G. "Pretend play: An integrative review." *Child Development*, Vol.52 (1981), pp. 1095-1118.
157. Parsons, trans. Max Weber, *The Protestant Work Ethic and the Spirit of Capitalism* (New York: Charles Scribner's Sons, 1905) pg. 105, 117.
158. See, for instance, Jane Bennett, *The Enchantment of Modern Life*, Jason Joseph-Storm's *The Myth of Disenchantment*, and Joshua Landy and Michael Saler's *The Re-Enchantment of the World*.
159. A.A. Milne, *The House at Pooh Corner* (McLellan and Stewart, 1928), pp. 1733, 178.
160. As popularised by the writer Anaïs Nin, *Seduction of the Minotaur* (1961), and the self-help author Steven Covey.
161. Abraham Maslow, *The Psychology of Science* (New York and London: Harper & Row, 1966) pg.15-16.
162. Arguably, it goes back to Immanuel Kant, but let's not complicate the picture too much.
163. It is also possible that the inspiration of a muse, or the assistance of an ancestor or a patron deity may also be involved. For the sake of the present argument, we shall lay this aside; the concept of *aletheia* as we receive it from the Western philosophical tradition neither excludes it nor requires a dimension of magic.
164. Heidegger, "The Question Concerning Technology", in *Basic Writings*, (Harper Collins, 1977) pg. 318.
165. Heidegger, *ibid*, pg. 326.
166. Heidegger, p. 330.
167. Heidegger, *ibid*, pg. 332. Emphasis added.
168. Heidegger, *ibid*, pg. 320. Emphasis added.
169. Heidegger, *ibid*, pg. 322.

170. Heidegger, *ibid*, pg. 339.

171. Michael Mann, Zhihua Zhang, Malcolm Hughes, et.al., "Proxy-based reconstructions of hemispheric and global surface temperature variations over the past two millennia." *Proceedings of the National Academy of Sciences,* Sept. 2008, 105 (36) 13252-13257.

172. Paul Crutzen, "Geology of Mankind", *Nature*, 415, 23 (2002).

173. Data from the online database published by the Food and Agriculture Organization of the United Nations. http://www.fao.org/faostat/en/#home Retrieved in June 2021.

174. Klein Goldewijk, K., A. Beusen, J. Doelman and E. Stehfest. "New anthropogenic land use estimates for the Holocene". *History Database of the Global Environment (HYDE 3.2)*, PBL Netherlands Environmental Assessment Agency, in prep. https://www.pbl.nl/en/image/links/hyde Retrieved in June 2021.

175. Stephens, L., Fuller, D., Boivin, N., et.al, (2019). "Archaeological assessment reveals Earth's early transformation through land use." *Science*, 365(6456), 897-902; Kump, L. R., Kasting, J. F., & Crane, R. G. (2004). *The Earth System* (Vol. 432). Upper Saddle River, NJ: Pearson Prentice Hall.

176. Mather, A. S., Fairbairn, J., & Needle, C. L. (1999). The course and drivers of the forest transition: the case of France. *Journal of Rural Studies*, 15(1), 65-90; Mather, A. S., & Needle, C. L. (2000). The relationships of population and forest trends. *Geographical Journal*, 166(1), 2-13; Hosonuma, N., Herold, M., De Sy, V., et.al., (2012). An assessment of deforestation and forest degradation drivers in developing countries. *Environmental Research Letters*, 7(4), 044009.

177. Fiona Grant, *Analysis of a Peat Core from the Clwydian Hills, North Wales.* Report of the Royal Commission on the Ancient and Historical Monuments of Wales, 2009; see also

George Monbiot, *Feral: Rewilding the Land, Sea, and Human Life*. (London: Penguin, 2013), pg. 66-69.

178. Ibrahim, Y.S., Tuan Anuar, S., Azmi, A.A., et.al., (2021), "Detection of microplastics in human colectomy specimens". *JGH Open*, 5: 116-121; Schwabl P, Köppel S, Königshofer P et al. "Detection of various microplastics in human stool: a prospective case series." *Ann. Intern. Med.* 2019; 171: 453-7; A.D. Vethaak, Juliette Legler. "Microplastics and human health" *Science*, Vol.371, Issue 6530, pp. 672-674. 12th February 2021.

179. United Nations Dept. of Economic and Social Affairs. *World Urbanization Prospects*, 2018.

180. United Nations: *The World's Cities in 2018: Data Booklet*, 2018. Data from ibid, *World Urbanization Prospects*, 2018.

181. Cited in Harries, *The Ethical Function of Architecture*, pg. 229.

182. Cited in Harries, *ibid*, pg. 338.

183. Harries, *The Ethical Function of Architecture*, pg. 231, 358.

184. BP Statistical Review of Global energy (2019).

185. Robin McKie, "Earth has lost 20 trillion tonnes of ice in less than 30 years" *The Guardian*, 23 August 2020.

186. Secretariat of the Convention on Biological Diversity, *Global Biodiversity Outlook 5 - Summary for Policy Makers*. (Montréal, 2020), pg. 2.

187. Hiroko Tabuchi, "A Secret Recording Reveals Oil Executives' Private Views on Climate Change" *The New York Times*, 12 September, 2020.

188. Hiroko Tabuchi, "In Video, Exxon Lobbyist Describes Efforts To Undercut Climate Action" *The New York Times*, 30th June, 2021.

189. Jessie Yeung, "Australia's deadly wildfires are showing no signs of stopping. Here's what you need to know." *CNN*, 2nd January 2020; Calla Wahlquist, "Mothers, daughters, fathers, sons: the victims of the Australian bushfires" *The*

Guardian, 3rd January 2020.

190. Ben Smee, "Darkness at noon: Australia's bushfire day of terror" *The Guardian*, 31 December 2019.

191. Kate Ng, "Australia wildfires: Half a billion animals and plants killed as glaciers turn black." *The Independent*, 2nd January 2020.

192. Irena Ceranic, "As heatwave bakes Australia on land, an unprecedented marine heatwave causes fish kills in the ocean." *Australia Broadcasting Corporation*, 18 December 2019.

193. Eleanor Ainge Roy, "New Zealand glaciers turn brown from Australian bushfires' smoke, ash and dust." *The Guardian*, 2nd January 2020.

194. "Recent projections of fire weather suggest that fire seasons will start earlier, end slightly later, and generally be more intense. This effect increases over time, but should be directly observable by 2020." Ross Garnaut, *The Garnaut Climate Change Review: Final Report.* (Commonwealth of Australia / Cambridge University Press, 2008), pg. 118.

195. Ross Garnaut, "Summary", in *Garnaut Climate Change Review - Update 2011*, (www.garnautreview.org.au), 31 May 2011, pg. 8.

196. Staff writers, "Scott Morrison heckled after he tries to shake hands with bushfire victim in NSW town of Cobargo" *The Guardian*, 2nd January 2020; Amy Remeikis, "PM Scott Morrison defends climate policies and asks Australians to be 'patient' over fires" *The Guardian*, 2nd January 2020; Amy Remeikis, "'No better place to raise kids': Scott Morrison's new year message to a burning Australia" *The Guardian*, 31 December 2019.

197. Staff writers, "Australia's leaders unmoved on climate action after devastating bushfires" *Reuters*, 7th January 2020.

198. Christopher Knaus, "Bots and trolls spread false arson

claims in Australian fires 'disinformation campaign'", *The Guardian*, 7th January 2020.

199. International Panel on Climate Change, 2018: "Summary for Policymakers." In: *Global Warming of 1.5°C. An IPCC Special Report on the impacts of global warming of 1.5°C above pre-industrial levels and related global greenhouse gas emission pathways, in the context of strengthening the global response to the threat of climate change, sustainable development, and efforts to eradicate poverty* [Masson-Delmotte, V., P. Zhai, H.-O. Pörtner, D. Roberts, J. Skea, P.R. Shukla, A. Pirani, W. Moufouma-Okia, C. Péan, R. Pidcock, S. Connors, J.B.R. Matthews, Y. Chen, X. Zhou, M.I. Gomis, E. Lonnoy, T. Maycock, M. Tignor, and T. Waterfield (eds.)]. In Press.

200. Jesse Winter, "Lululemon founder buys Canadian islands to conserve ecosystems" *The Guardian*, 30 June 2021.

201. Mark O'Connell, "Why Silicon Valley billionaires are prepping for the apocalypse in New Zealand" *The Guardian*, 15th February 2018.

202. Olivia Solon, "Elon Musk: we must colonise Mars to preserve our species in a third world war" *The Guardian*, 11 March 2018.

203. Lin, Wambersie, and Wackernagel, *Estimating the Date of Earth Overshoot Day 2021*. Press release by Global Footprint Network, May 2021. URL: https://www.overshootday.org/content/uploads/2021/06/Earth-Overshoot-Day-2021-Nowcast-Report.pdf

204. Cunsolo, A. & Ellis, N. R. (2018). Ecological grief as a mental health response to climate change-related loss. *Nature Climate Change, 8*(4), pg. 275.

205. Ashlee Cunsolo, et.al., "You can never replace the caribou: Inuit experiences of Ecological Grief from Caribou Declines" *American Imago*, Vol.77 No.1, Spring 2020, pp. 31-59.

206. Clayton, S. (2018). Mental health risk and resilience among

climate scientists. *Nature Climate Change, 8,* 260-271; see also: Clayton, S., Manning, C. M., Krygsman, K., & Speiser, M. (2017). *Mental Health and Our Changing Climate: Impacts, Implications, and Guidance.* Washington, D.C.: American Psychological Association, and ecoAmerica.

207. Hundertwasser, *Mould Manifesto against Rationalism in Architecture,* 1958.

208. Harries, *ibid,* pg. 236.

209. Heidegger, "The Question Concerning Technology", in *Basic Writings,* (Harper Collins, 1977), pg. 329.

210. Heidegger, ibid, pg. 332. Emphasis added.

211. Heidegger, *ibid,* pg. 332.

212. Alex Mistlin, "Human consumption of the Earth's resources declined in 2020" *The Guardian,* 21 August 2020.

213. Matt Bubbers, "In Canada and cities around the world, rush-hour traffic plummets as people respond to the COVID-19 pandemic" *The Globe And Mail,* 24 March 2020.

214. Tamara Thiessen, "40% Less Flights Worldwide: This Is What's Happening With Air Travel" *Forbes,* 1st April 2020.

215. IP Singh, "Photos: Seen from Jalandhar rooftops, Dhauladhar in full glory" *The Times of India,* 4th April 2020.

216. Ellis-Peterson, Ratcliffe, Cowie, Daniels, and Kuo, "'It's positively alpine!': Disbelief in big cities as air pollution falls" *The Guardian,* 11 April 2020.

217. Drew Kann, "Los Angeles has notoriously polluted air. But right now it has some of the cleanest of any major city". *CNN,* 7th April 2020.

218. The editors, "Will this pandemic's legacy be a universal basic income?" *MacLean's,* 19th May 2020.

219. Corrine LeQuéré, et.al., "Temporary reduction in daily global CO_2 emissions during the COVID-19 forced confinement" *Nature Climate Change,* 19th May 2020.

220. PA Media, "Carbon dioxide levels in atmosphere reach

record high" *The Guardian* (citing data published by the Scripps Institution of Oceanography, University of San Diego), 7th April 2021.

221. James Conca, "Can we make a nuclear reactor that won't melt down?" *Forbes*, 24 January 2018. See also: H. van Dam, "The Self-stabilizing Criticality Wave Reactor", *Proc. Of the Tenth International Conference on Emerging Nuclear Energy Systems (ICENES 2000)*, p. 188, NRG, Petten, Netherlands (2000).

222. Kikstra, Mastrucci, Min, et.al., "Decent living gaps and energy needs around the world" *Environmental Letters Research*, Vol.16 (September 2021), 095006.

223. Stephen R. Gliessman, *Agroecology: The Ecology of Sustainable Food Systems*. 3rd Edition. (CRC Press, 2014); see also IPCC, *Climate Change 2014 Mitigation of Climate Change: Working Group III Contribution to the Fifth Assessment Report of the Intergovernmental Panel on Climate Change*. (Cambridge University Press, 2014.) See also: Altieri, Miguel A, and Clara Nicholls. 2012. "The Scaling up of Agroecology: Spreading the Hope for Food Sovereignty and Resiliency. A Contribution to Discussions at Rio + 20 on Issues at the Interface of Hunger, Agriculture, Environment and Social." In *Rio +20*. See also: Badgley, Moghtader, Quintero, et.al., "Organic Agriculture and the Global Food Supply." *Renewable Agriculture and Food Systems* 22(2), 2007, pp. 86-108.

224. Jillian Kestler-D'Amours, "This river in Canada is now a 'legal person'" *Al Jazeera*, 3rd April 2021; Mihnea Tanasescu, "Rivers Get Human Rights: They Can Sue To Protect Themselves" *Scientific American / The Conversation*, 19th June 2017.

225. Kevin Michael Deluca, "Thinking with Heidegger: Rethinking environmental theory and practice" *Ethics and The Environment*, 10(1), 2005, pp. 67-87.

226. Heidegger, "The Origin of the Work of Art". *Basic Writings*, pg. 171-2.

227. "It is a fundamental mistake to suppose that amoeba or infusoria are more imperfect or incomplete animals than elephants or apes... Thus nature, whether it is lifeless nature or indeed living nature, is in no way to be regarded as the plank or lowest rung of the ladder which the human being would ascend." Heidegger, *The Fundamental Concepts of Metaphysics: World, Finitude, Solitude*. Trans. William McNeil and Nicholas Walker. (Bloomington, IN, USA: Indiana University Press, 1999) pp. 287.

228. Heidegger, *ibid*, pg. 337.

229. See, for instance, Luc Ferry and Alain Renaut, *Heidegger and Modernity* (Chicago: U of Chicago Press, 1990), pp. 65-68.

230. Cited in Thomas Sheehan, "Heidegger and the Nazis", *New York Review Of Books*, 16th June 1988, pg. 45.

231. Martin Heidegger, "Nur noch ein Gott kann uns retten," *Der Spiegel* 30 Mai, 1976: 193-219. Trans. by W. Richardson as "Only a God Can Save Us" in *Heidegger: The Man and the Thinker* (1981), ed. T. Sheehan, pp. 45-67.

232. Paul Hockenos, "Release of Heidegger's 'Black Notebooks' Reignites Debate Over Nazi Ideology" *The Chronicle of Higher Education*, 24th February 2014. Ecologists who want the help of a phenomenologist should look to Hans Jonas instead.

233. Garland Allen, "Culling the Herd: Eugenics and the Conservation Movement in the United States, 1900-1940" *Journal of the History of Biology*, March 2021; Jedediah Purdy, "Environmentalism's Racist History", *The New Yorker*, 13 August 2015.

234. Hardin's "harsh ethics of the lifeboat" depends, in every step in its logic, on "overpopulated" countries stabilizing their numbers through the death-by-neglect of large masses

of their people. "Without some system of worldwide food sharing, the proportion of people in the rich and poor nations might eventually stabilize. The overpopulated poor countries would decrease in numbers [ie, the poor must die], while the rich countries that had room for more people would increase. But with a well-meaning system of sharing, such as a world food bank, the growth differential between the rich and the poor countries will not only persist, it will increase." Objections to this view are represented in his essay using hyperbolic straw-man language, and dismissed as absurdities. Hardin, "Lifeboat Ethics: The Case Against Helping The Poor" *Psychology Today*, September 1974.

235. Brenton Tarrant, 'The Great Replacement', 2019. See also: Andreas Malm and the Zetkin Collective, *White Skin, Black Fuel: On the Danger of Fossil Fascism* (London: Verso, 2021), pp. 151-2; Kathy Gilsinan, "How White-Supremacist Violence Echoes Other Forms of Terrorism" *The Atlantic*, 15th March 2019; Luke Darby, "How the 'Great Replacement' conspiracy theory has inspired white supremacist killers" *The Telegraph*, 5th August 2019.

236. Motesharrei, Rivas, and Kalnay: "Human and Nature Dynamics (HANDY) Modeling Inequality and Use of Resources in the Collapse or Sustainability of Societies", *Ecological Economics* Vol. 101, May 2014, pp.90-102.

237. This definition of *need* follows McMurtry, *Unequal Freedoms*, as cited earlier.

238. Brendan Montague, "Polluters banned from COP26 public venues" *The Ecologist*, 20th August 2021; see also Glasgow City Council Agenda, item 9(b), 1st April 2021. https://www.glasgow.gov.uk/councillorsandcommittees/agenda.asp?meetingid=17375

239. Haroon Siddique, "Legal experts draw up 'historic' definition of ecocide" *The Guardian*, 22 June 2021.

240. Staff writers, "Educating Girls may Be Nigeria's Best Hope Against Climate Change" *Sierra* Club, Nov/Dec 2019, pg. 1-11; Vanessa Nakate, "How Educating Girls Will Help Combat The Climate Crisis" *Time*, 14th April 2021; Natu Rashidi Msuya, "Economic Benefits of Educating Girls in Developing Countries" *Conference Proceedings of the G20 Youth Forum*, 2014, Issue 2, p. 551-562.

241. Although I regard this as a fully ecocentric model of ethics, the argument also works from an anthropocentric view. For our own lives remain dependent on the Earth and its systems, its music. If we kill the musician, we too may die. If we *stress* the musician, that is to say if we enclose much or most but not all of the Earth into the frame of the human without respecting its carrying capacities and other boundaries, then the music changes, that is to say the system comes ever-closer to tipping points beyond which it may change to a state that is unsurvivable for humans. In this view, respecting the Earth as a complex system translates into practice as respecting its carrying capacities and avoiding interference in its ecological systems, as well as all the other proposals I'm offering here.

242. This expands upon arguments by Emmanuel Lévinas, who in *Time And The Other* (1947) argued that ethics arises from the gaze of the Other: the gaze which "forbids murder" and "commands justice" because it cannot be grasped. The Earth, as an immensity, obviously does not 'gaze' in this way. In the logical place of the gaze, the Earth presents us with an ungraspable complex of systems and emergent properties. It should be clear how this phenomenology of complex systems challenges Heidegger's notion of 'granting'. For in Heidegger's argument, things grant themselves to us without regard for how that granting affects human *eudaimonia,* nor how it affects the complex systems from which things are taken, nor how the act of

enframing kills that which is enframed. Heidegger's view is irreducibly anthropocentric.

243. Kate Raworth, *Doughnut Economics: Seven Ways to Think Like a 21st Century Economist* (Random House, 2017).

244. Jean-Paul Rodrigue, *The Geography of Transport Systems*, 5th Edition. (New York: Routledge, 2020), chapter 8.2.

245. Valiente, *The Charge of the Goddess*, 1954.

246. See for example: Stellar, J. E., Gordon, A., Anderson, C. L., Piff, P. K., McNeil, G. D., & Keltner, D. (2018). "Awe and humility". *Journal of personality and social psychology, 114*(2), 258-269; see also Darcher Keltner and Jonathan Haidt, "Approaching Awe, a moral, spiritual, and aesthetic emotion" *Cognition and Emotion*, 2003, 17(2), 297-314.

Other books in the Earth Spirit series

Belonging to the Earth
Nature Spirituality in a Changing World
Julie Brett
978-1-78904-969-5 (Paperback)
978-1-78904-970-1 (ebook)

Confronting the Crisis
Essays and Meditations on Eco-Spirituality
David Sparenberg
978-1-78904-973-2 (Paperback)
978-1-78904-974-9 (ebook)

Eco-Spirituality and Human–Animal Relationships
Through an Ethical and Spiritual Lens
Mark Hawthorne
978-1-78535-248-5 (Paperback)
978-1-78535-249-2 (ebook)

Environmental Gardening
Think Global Act Local
Elen Sentier
978-1-78904-963-3 (Paperback)
978-1-78904-964-0 (ebook)

Healthy Planet
Global Meltdown or Global Healing
Fred Hageneder
978-1-78904-830-8 (Paperback)
978-1-78904-831-5 (ebook)

Honoring the Wild

Reclaiming Witchcraft and Environmental Activism

Irisanya Moon

978-1-78904-961-9 (Paperback)

978-1-78904-962-6 (ebook)

Saving Mother Ocean

We all need to help save the seas!

Steve Andrews

978-1-78904-965-7 (Paperback)

978-1-78904-966-4 (ebook)

**MOON
BOOKS**

PAGANISM & SHAMANISM

What is Paganism? A religion, a spirituality, an alternative belief system, nature worship? You can find support for all these definitions (and many more) in dictionaries, encyclopaedias, and text books of religion, but subscribe to any one and the truth will evade you. Above all Paganism is a creative pursuit, an encounter with reality, an exploration of meaning and an expression of the soul. Druids, Heathens, Wiccans and others, all contribute their insights and literary riches to the Pagan tradition. Moon Books invites you to begin or to deepen your own encounter, right here, right now.

If you have enjoyed this book, why not tell other readers by posting a review on your preferred book site.

Recent bestsellers from Moon Books are:

Journey to the Dark Goddess
How to Return to Your Soul
Jane Meredith
Discover the powerful secrets of the Dark Goddess and
transform your depression, grief and pain into healing
and integration.
Paperback: 978-1-84694-677-6 ebook: 978-1-78099-223-5

Shamanic Reiki
Expanded Ways of Working with Universal Life Force Energy
Llyn Roberts, Robert Levy
Shamanism and Reiki are each powerful ways of healing; together,
their power multiplies. *Shamanic Reiki* introduces techniques to
help healers and Reiki practitioners tap ancient healing wisdom.
Paperback: 978-1-84694-037-8 ebook: 978-1-84694-650-9

Pagan Portals – The Awen Alone
Walking the Path of the Solitary Druid
Joanna van der Hoeven
An introductory guide for the solitary Druid, *The Awen Alone* will
accompany you as you explore, and seek out your own place
within the natural world.
Paperback: 978-1-78279-547-6 ebook: 978-1-78279-546-9

A Kitchen Witch's World of Magical Herbs & Plants
Rachel Patterson
A journey into the magical world of herbs and plants, filled with
magical uses, folklore, history and practical magic. By popular
writer, blogger and kitchen witch, Tansy Firedragon.
Paperback: 978-1-78279-621-3 ebook: 978-1-78279-620-6

Medicine for the Soul
The Complete Book of Shamanic Healing
Ross Heaven
All you will ever need to know about shamanic healing and how to
become your own shaman...
Paperback: 978-1-78099-419-2 ebook: 978-1-78099-420-8

Shaman Pathways – The Druid Shaman
Exploring the Celtic Otherworld
Danu Forest
A practical guide to Celtic shamanism with exercises and
techniques as well as traditional lore for exploring the Celtic
Otherworld.
Paperback: 978-1-78099-615-8 ebook: 978-1-78099-616-5

Traditional Witchcraft for the Woods and Forests
A Witch's Guide to the Woodland with Guided Meditations and
Pathworking
Mélusine Draco
A Witch's guide to walking alone in the woods, with guided
meditations and pathworking.
Paperback: 978-1-84694-803-9 ebook: 978-1-84694-804-6

Wild Earth, Wild Soul
A Manual for an Ecstatic Culture
Bill Pfeiffer
Imagine a nature-based culture so alive and so connected,
spreading like wildfire. This book is the first flame...
Paperback: 978-1-78099-187-0 ebook: 978-1-78099-188-7

Naming the Goddess
Trevor Greenfield
Naming the Goddess is written by over eighty adherents and
scholars of Goddess and Goddess Spirituality.
Paperback: 978-1-78279-476-9 ebook: 978-1-78279-475-2

Shapeshifting into Higher Consciousness
Heal and Transform Yourself and Our World with Ancient
Shamanic and Modern Methods
Llyn Roberts
Ancient and modern methods that you can use every day to
transform yourself and make a positive difference in the world.
Paperback: 978-1-84694-843-5 ebook: 978-1-84694-844-2

Readers of ebooks can buy or view any of these bestsellers by
clicking on the live link in the title. Most titles are published in
paperback and as an ebook. Paperbacks are available in traditional
bookshops. Both print and ebook formats are available online.

Find more titles and sign up to our readers' newsletter at
http://www.johnhuntpublishing.com/paganism
Follow us on Facebook at https://www.facebook.com/MoonBooks
and Twitter at https://twitter.com/MoonBooksJHP